FISHERS OF MEN

EVOLVER

AN EVOLVER BOOK

FISHERS OF MEN

THE GOSPEL OF AN AYAHUASCA VISION QUEST

ADAM ELENBAAS

JEREMY P. TARCHER/PENGUIN

a member of Penguin Group (USA) Inc.

New York

JEREMY P. TARCHER/PENGUIN
Published by the Penguin Group
Penguin Group (USA) Inc., 375 Hudson Street, New York, New York 10014,
USA • Penguin Group (Canada), 90 Eglinton Avenue East, Suite 700, Toronto,
Ontario M4P 2Y3, Canada (a division of Pearson Penguin Canada Inc.) • Penguin Books Ltd,
80 Strand, London WC2R 0RL, England • Penguin Ireland, 25 St Stephen's Green, Dublin 2,
Ireland (a division of Penguin Books Ltd) • Penguin Group (Australia), 250 Camberwell Road,
Camberwell, Victoria 3124, Australia (a division of Pearson Australia Group Pty Ltd) •
Penguin Books India Pvt Ltd, 11 Community Centre, Panchsheel Park,
New Delhi–110 017, India • Penguin Group (NZ), 67 Apollo Drive, Rosedale, North Shore
0632, New Zealand (a division of Pearson New Zealand Ltd) • Penguin Books
(South Africa) (Pty) Ltd, 24 Sturdee Avenue, Rosebank, Johannesburg 2196, South Africa

Penguin Books Ltd, Registered Offices: 80 Strand, London WC2R 0RL, England

Most Tarcher/Penguin books are available at special quantity discounts for bulk purchase for
sales promotions, premiums, fund-raising, and educational needs. Special books or book
excerpts also can be created to fit specific needs. For details, write Penguin Group (USA) Inc.
Special Markets, 375 Hudson Street, New York, NY 10014.

Library of Congress Cataloging-in-Publication Data
Elenbaas, Adam.
Fishers of men: the gospel of an ayahuasca vision quest / Adam Elenbaas.
p.   cm.
ISBN 978-1-58542-791-8
1. Elenbaas, Adam.   2. Spiritual biography.   3. Hallucinogenic drugs and religious
experience—South America.   4 Ayahuasca ceremony—South America.   5. Shamanism—
South America.   I. Title.
BL73.E44A3   2010   2010005030
299.8' 138092—dc22

Printed in the United States of America
1   3   5   7   9   10   8   6   4   2

BOOK DESIGN BY NICOLE LAROCHE

Neither the publisher nor the author is engaged in rendering professional advice or services
to the individual reader. The ideas, procedures, and suggestions contained in this book are
not intended as a substitute for consulting with a physician. All matters regarding your
health require medical supervision. Neither the author nor the publisher shall be liable or
responsible for any loss or damage allegedly arising from any information or suggestion in
this book.

While the author has made every effort to provide accurate telephone numbers and Internet
addresses at the time of publication, neither the publisher nor the author assumes any
responsibility for errors, or for changes that occur after publication. Further, the publisher
does not have any control over and does not assume any responsibility for author or third-
party websites or their content.

Penguin is committed to publishing works of quality and integrity.
In that spirit, we are proud to offer this book to our readers;
however, the story, the experiences, and the words
are the author's alone.

CONTENTS

There is a magic intoxicant in northwesternmost South America which the Indians believe can free the soul from corporeal confinement, allowing it to wander free and return to the body at will. The soul, thus untrammeled, liberates its owner from the realities of everyday life and introduces him to wondrous realms of what he considers reality and permits him to communicate with his ancestors. The Quechua term for this inebriating drink—Ayahuasca ("vine of the soul")—refers to this freeing of the spirit. The plants involved are truly plants of the gods, for their power is laid to supernatural forces residing in their tissues, and they were divine gifts to the earliest Indians on earth.

—Richard Evans Schultes, Albert Hofmann, and
  Christian Rätsch, *Plants of the Gods: Their Sacred,
  Healing, and Hallucinogenic Powers*

This is a true story. Some names and locales have been changed to protect the privacy of people involved, and at certain points time lines were condensed or slightly altered for the sake of the narrative.

CHAPTER 1

GOD'S BATHROOM FLOOR

I stood at the door and knocked.

"You okay?"

Groans came from inside. The morning sunlight shone brightly through the parsonage windows. I knocked again. There was no response.

"Dad?"

My father cried and sniffled behind the door. His breathing was irregular. I opened the door slowly. He sat on the floor near the toilet. His face was a tangled mess of tears and leathery wrinkles. He held out his right arm for me to see. It was covered in patches of blood. In his fist he clutched a deer-hunting knife. He looked at me for a moment in silence. Saliva bubbled between his lips.

"Am I okay?" he asked me. He gestured to me with his bloody arm, palm facing up and fingers limp, his other hand gripping the knife.

Everything slowed down. My body shrank to the floor. I sat on my knees. I didn't know what to say. I thought of all the times in the past month I had found my dad doubled over behind the toilet bowl crying or shaking.

I could usually talk him down to firm ground again. I had thought to myself on a number of such occasions, *He's going to kill himself one of these times.*

He was withdrawing from his cocktail of antidepressants, sleep aids, and antianxiety medications. He quit taking them cold turkey. He wouldn't listen to anybody who told him to take it easy on himself, to take one step at a time. He wanted healing, and he was going to Peru, as I had, on a vision quest. He had to be off his medications first in order to drink ayahuasca.

"Am I okay?" he asked me again. He brought his face close to mine. His eyelids fluttered and twitched.

Blood dripped onto the white tiles.

The sunlight pooled and a breeze passed through the windows, blowing the curtains back.

I imagined all of the times I had heard my father, a Methodist minister, preach Sunday morning sermons from the pulpit. I imagined the entire church congregation sitting on that bathroom floor, right there with me, hushed, sitting in a circle around him, the men with their ties finally loosened, shirts untucked, and the women sitting Indian style, their summer dresses shining in the morning sun, everybody listening carefully, everybody witnessing my father's best sermon to date.

I tried to think of how to answer his question, *"Am I okay?"* but nothing came immediately. Nothing came easily. Only the steady rhythm of my breathing and his.

CHAPTER 2

TAKE THIS CUP

One lantern was lit in the mesa. The jungle lurched and bent with cackling birdcalls and bullfrog croaks in the lagoon. Thunderclouds rumbled above the canopy of the forest, and a small lodge dog named Cucaracha snored underneath the awning of the screen door. Six of us sat in a circle. A master shaman of El Puma Negro Healing Lodge, an American named Ethan Richter, sang medicine songs into the ceremonial tin cup, invoking the chief medicinal plant spirits of the jungle. I had met Ethan two days before the first ceremony.

"Welcome to El Puma Negro. This is my home," Ethan had said to us as our canoes came to rest against the bank of a murky, green lagoon. El Puma Negro lodge sat on the top of a hill overlooking the river.

When I first arrived in Iquitos, Peru, I had expected Ethan's teachers, mestizo shamans named Domingo and Arturo, to lead the ayahuasca ceremonies. Even though Ethan assured us that he had completed a rigorous apprenticeship and had been granted the title of Maestro by his teachers and their lineage, I felt skeptical when I learned that Arturo and Domingo would be absent for the ceremonies. Having come to the Amazon for the healing effects and transcendental visions of the mystical entheogen traditionally called *huasca* or *the yage* but more popularly ayahuasca, and having only read books and magazine articles about the shamanic traditions of the Amazon (using ayahuasca is illegal in the United States), my intention was to have a sacred, and not recreational, psychedelic experience, something like a vision quest or primitive rite of passage. I was therefore apprehensive about Ethan's shamanic qualifications. Certainly a white man leading the ceremonies meant I was not guaranteed the "real" ayahuasca experience. But after traveling nearly twenty-four hours from the United States to the jungle outpost city of Iquitos, and after listening to Ethan speak eloquently about his ayahuasca apprenticeship on the ferry carrying us upriver from Iquitos into the jungle, I was appeased enough to let the white man into a tradition I (a white man) knew next to nothing about anyway.

When we collected the ingredients for the ayahuasca medicine along the banks of the river, Ethan had scurried up a tree barefoot, cutting a section of bark off with a machete and then blessing the wound and treating it with *mapacho* (sacred tobacco) smoke.

"Arturo and Domingo will be at the ceremonies in spirit this week," Ethan said, as if sensing my uncertainty. "El Puma Negro is on their family land," he added.

I was the first to drink in the mesa (the ceremonial circle). In the dim light of the lantern flame the ayahuasca tea was brown and red, like syrup and mud stirred together. Ethan invited each one of us to say a prayer or voice an intention before we drank. Silently in my head I said the words "humble me."

"*¡Salud!*" Ethan cried. I tipped back the tin cup and swallowed three big gulps of warm ayahuasca, only half a cup. Everybody in the ceremonial circle echoed his cry, "*¡Salud!*"

By the time the cup finished around the circle and everybody had drunk, I felt uneasy. Ethan blew out the lantern flame and shook his *chakapa* (leaf rattle). In the dark I saw the glowing tip of his *mapacho* cigar pulsing red and black, red and black. Then he sang an *icaro*, a traditional medicine song. The strange melody that emptied out of his mouth was different from anything I'd ever heard. Unraveling before me, it seemed a language unto itself. For twenty minutes I listened uneasily to the medicine song, shifting back and forth on my mattress pad nervously, waiting to feel the effects of the ayahuasca.

First, I felt a warm tingling in my stomach, slow and nauseating, and then in my arms, moving faster and working its way up to the crown of my skull. Then my entire body felt watery and increasingly sensitive, the smallest movements spreading through me like sound waves bouncing through a tunnel, until my body felt light as a feather and I could see faint lights growing brighter and brighter, forming geometric shapes and colors, swimming through the air like mercury, a crystal-clear tapestry of mixing sounds and images that moved as one.

I sat cross-legged on my mattress pad watching the colors for what felt like hours but was only minutes. The shapes turned to elements of nature. I saw sketchy outlines of star systems and planets, supernovae and galaxies, then into the earth among mountains and rivers, volcanoes and deserts, soaring like an eagle. Then as if the song had found its way from the farthest reaches of space to the exact location of the mesa on top of a hill in the Amazon jungle of Peru, I saw animals from the rain forest—snakes and jaguars, parrots and spiders, pink river dolphins and monkeys—and green vines descending into the mesa.

"Welcome to your first ayahuasca ceremony, everybody," Ethan said. Then he sang again.

I tracked the song back to Ethan's mouth. The icaro medicine song was not being sung by a person to an audience, but rather it was channeled. I saw Ethan as a giant man with a golden hornet's face, his *chakapa* rattle beating out a trance rhythm, his human personality gone and his mouth wide open, body unhinged, shoulders back, head tilted back, and the visionary song pouring out of his mouth like molten lava rushing down the rocks.

My body and all of my perceptions melted into the vision-producing *icaro*. Just as the *icaro* became the colors and shapes, the shapes changing into images, and just as Ethan transformed into the *icaro* itself, I, too, merged into the visions and music. A panic rose into my chest.

What have I done? I thought to myself. *Am I going to lose it?*

My questions left me like water and streamlined into visions. The question "What have I done?" repeated itself over and over again, the sounds of the words and syllables warped and shimmered, speeding up and slowing down. A trail of spectacular colors moved above my head.

Then I saw an old man on his knees in the center of the mesa. He raised his hands to the sky with a desperate look on his face. It was as if my question, "What have I done?" had been transformed into a universal symbol. No sooner did my question merge into the medicine song and vision soup than the answer came in another vision. I saw the old man on the ground again, this time shaking and screaming. The image floated above me in the mesa. His hands on his face. His neck and head seizing violently. His mouth opening wide and his body collapsing into convulsions. All the while I heard my question in his expressions: "What have I done? What have I done?"

"*Shoooo. Shooooo.*" Ethan blew sharply through his mouth.

As soon as he blew through his lips, *shoooo, shoooo,* a dragon soared into the mesa, opened its mouth, and swallowed the image of the old man. I burped loudly, and a swamp-sized cloud of gas released from somewhere deep inside my body. Then the dragon spit the old man out, like regurgitated food. When the old man emerged from the mouth of the serpent, he was clothed in sparkling jewels. A look of peace on his face. He looked at me and said, "Trust yourself. Your truth is always within you." Diamonds and stars descended gently through the mesa, perfectly aligned with the rhythm of Ethan's *chakapa* and magical *icaro* song.

It could have taken years to realize how frequently my questions were statements and my statements cynical. Although I had phrased them as questions—"What have I done? Am I going to lose it?"—I had said something direct. I had said to myself, "I have done the wrong thing, and I am afraid to lose control." I lay down and exhaled deeply. As if countless hours of invaluable psychotherapy had occurred instantly, the entire time I watched my question transform itself into the image of the old man and then emerge from the mouth of the dragon, a matter of sheer minutes had passed.

As my second rhetorical question, "Am I going to lose it?" unfolded into the soup of mesa visions and *icaro* music, it was clear that others in the mesa shared my fear. Several people moaned, and somebody burped. The human noises in the mesa said, "We're losing control!" The medicine boiled inside us. Ethan's *icaro* picked up. I curled into the fetal position. The visions moved faster.

CHAPTER 3

LIMBO IN LYDIA

In the New Testament Book of Acts, Lydia was a widowed merchant of purple cloth. The color purple in the Greek Mediterranean symbolized royalty. In the Greek language of the New Testament Lydia was called a worshipper of God. This meant Lydia was an outsider, commonly called a gentile, who worshipped the Jewish God by choice not tradition. She became famous for converting to Christianity and secretly housing the outlaw Christian preacher, Paul, who baptized Lydia at her home near Philippi as he traveled across the Mediterranean writing the New Testament epistles.

Shortly after Paul's conversion visit with Lydia and her baptism, he was imprisoned in Philippi with his companion, Silas, for breaking Roman regulations regarding his espousal of a universal Christian Gospel that transcended Roman religious authority. In Paul's evangelism to Lydia, there was no longer Jew or Gentile, male or female, Greek or Roman, but one true God of the universe, who lived within everything and all people, everywhere the same. Paul and Silas were said to have escaped Philippi when an earthquake destroyed their prison cell.

Just as Paul had converted Lydia—an outsider who worshipped the Jewish God until she accepted Paul's Universal God—my father, a Christian pastor, was committed to teaching his congregations in his first parish on the prairies of southern Minnesota, called Lydia United Methodist, why being a Christian should transcend the exclusive power structures of an institutional authority or church doctrine.

I remember evenings in Lydia, sitting on the porch of the church parsonage, which was built on the edge of a rolling cornfield. Hearing distant dog barks or the backfire of a muffler somewhere in the distance. My mother's voice in the still moments, saying "It's so quiet." My father looking up into the pink clouds, the purple sky, saying, "It's good to be alive."

Sundays the gravel lot in front of the sanctuary filled with station wagons and pickup trucks stacked high with wire chicken crates. My father wore a long, black robe. I waited in line with the adults to shake his hand after his sermon, after the benediction was finished and the last organ notes faded. When I shook his hand he shooed me away nervously, being sure to remain professional for the old folks. He said, "Okay, son. Find your mother. Have something to eat."

The choir hung their robes in the closets. The organist took off her eyeglasses and let them hang from their chain onto her wrinkly chest. Slowly, men in black suits and women in floral-patterned dresses filtered into the basement to eat hot-dish bean casserole and steaming trays of ham. Potlucks almost every Sunday. People filling their stomachs and gossiping.

I sat quietly, waiting for the time when the parking lot slowly cleared of the station wagons and pickup trucks. Then my mother walked me home across the prairie grass to the edge of the cornfield. She took a nap while I watched patiently from the parsonage window, waiting to see the figure of my father, his black robe put away, walking home to me through the tall green and white grass.

From early on at Lydia United Methodist I sensed the subtle tension between my father's and mother's roles as my parents and as pastor and preacher's wife. I remember how people looked at me next to my parents, too: the preacher's kid.

"Preacher's kids are trouble down the road, pastor. Keep your eye on him," a farmer said to my parents one morning.

My mother answered, "He's a good boy," as if she were really saying, "Back off, mister." My father smiled, adding, "We'll keep him straight," as if he were saying, "But thank you for your concern."

Thankfully, my boyhood revelations came not only from Methodism but also from Nature. My parents would wake me from my sleep and take me canoeing on Carl's Lake under the moonlight. My mother would make popcorn in the air popper and fill a brown paper grocery bag. My father would paddle us into the middle of the lake, my mother and I digging out handfuls of popcorn, my father reading stories from books, making special voices for each character (our own special ritual and our own sanctuary). The best stories he told were taken from collections of world mythology,

Native American folklore, and Romantic poetry, stories like *The Odyssey*, *The Rime of the Ancient Mariner*, Edgar Allan Poe's "The Raven," and *Black Elk Speaks*.

I remember one evening in particular, the way certain moments from earliest childhood must stay with you even to old age. I was only four years old, and my parents had taken me onto the lake in the canoe. It was springtime, and there was no moon in the sky.

"Why does the moon go away?" I asked.

"Well, it's just like everything," my dad said. "The moon rises and sets. It waxes and wanes. It gets big and full, and then it goes away until we can't see it. Then it comes back again."

A giant rock bass jumped out of the water and splashed back under. Then another and another. Splash after splash and the shining scales of silver fish in the night, the quiet lake became a frenzy under the stars.

"Daddy, Daddy, why are the fish trying to get out of the lake?"

"They're feeding on the flies," my dad answered. "The flies only live for a few hours," my dad said to himself, resting his paddle across his knees. "But they serve a purpose, don't they?"

"God's creation is quite mysterious," my mother replied. She breathed a deep and reverent sigh, as if she were looking at something far beyond where her eyes could see.

Compared to the inspirational contemplativeness of my parents, people at church seemed uninterested in mysteries like the stars and the moon. Christian rituals on Sundays were tiresome and dull in contrast to the curiosity I felt all the way down to my bones while sitting in the canoe at night. Increasingly, the paradox of these two worlds embossed themselves into my very DNA: the bright colors of the sky, legends and poetry, the silence of the prairies and rattle of the cornfields, but also the sermons and lifeless rituals in the sanctuary, people upright and tight behind suits and handshakes and gossip around tables about "sin," or how a certain farmer was "taking to the bottle" or "falling away from God again."

Over and over I tried diverting my parent's attention from church members during inappropriate moments. Raising my hand during a sermon. Tugging at my father's robe while he tried to speak to people after the worship service or asking my mother if we could go for a canoe ride in front of the parishioners, always trying to claim my turf, claim a sanctuary of my own.

One morning, while my mother taught children's Sunday school, I made my boldest attempt. I was five years old.

"Let's close our eyes and say a prayer, children," my mother said. While my mother closed her eyes and began to pray, "Dear God, we thank you for this beautiful morning," I scanned the room for children not closing their eyes. I spotted a young boy named Jeremiah. He picked his nose and wiped the boogers on his orange plastic chair. When my mother finished the prayer, I raised my hand urgently, kicking my legs back and forth.

"Mommy," I said. "Jeremiah didn't have his eyes closed during the prayer."

"How do you know he didn't have his eyes closed?" my mother asked me.

"Because I watched him," I said. "I saw him. He picked his boogers, and he didn't have his eyes closed."

"But for you to see him," my mother answered, "you must have had your eyes open, too." She smiled at me as if I were not her son but one of her students, the same as everybody else in the classroom. My lips quivered, and hot tears streamed down my face.

It was hard for me to understand the way in which my parents were both distant and separate from the parishioners in mood and affectation, but also among the people, trying to be the same as them and holding me, the preacher's kid, to the same rules as the parishioners. Naturally, as a young boy I felt in limbo, suspended between worlds of judgment and acceptance, rules and intuition, tradition and freedom, mystery and certainty. Since each world carried spiritual jargon and talk about God or the Holy Spirit, my impressions of Christianity were confusing. The very word *God* was a moving symbol for the different sanctuaries I inhabited. One sanctuary always seemed in competition with another, one trying to get love from a dry well, the other simply feeling loved, like fresh lake water throughout the seasons, always turning over.

For my parents, religious limbo was nothing new. Both late baby boomers, they had grown up inside more extreme versions of the same split identity. My mother's father, a World War II veteran and Detroit auto mechanic, died of cancer when my mother was twenty-one years old. Before my mother was born, my mother's mother, a Navy-trained WAVE and early feminist, was the first woman in her family to attend college. When she was offered her dream job as a newspaper journalist, members of my grandmother's church warned her that female reporters were all "floozies." Instead, she found a position as a primary-school instructor in Detroit, teaching impoverished minority children.

By the time my mother was born, her parents had survived the Great Depression as children, lived through the war, and were participating in public battles for both women's rights and affordable health care. Members of the Detroit Catholic Diocese, each career, family, and political decision reflected religious moods in the Catholic community. Having different personal ideas inevitably meant navigating many different religious and social structures. The public and private personas of my mother's family were constantly in flux.

At the same time in the northern Michigan countryside, my father was caught between the feuding of his parents. His father, a Korean War veteran, nasty drunk, unfaithful husband, workaholic, and chain smoker, and his mother, a country hymn–singing fundamentalist and *domestic* workaholic, my father received little affection in a world of social conventions and religious expectations. When my father was busted for possessing a bag of marijuana in high school, his father bailed him out of jail. After that, my grandfather's judgment of my father became angrier but more tacit. He formed harsher judgments about neo-spiritualism and the "hippie" socialist culture he assumed my father was part of. And when my dad finally moved out of the house, his father quit drinking and smoking cold turkey, and became born-again.

In the absence of his dad's guidance, my father spent time in the forests of northern Michigan with his best friends, some of whom were Pontiac Indian Boys. They would mimic the old tribal traditions, cutting their hands together with hunting knives, building their own tepees, and bestowing one another power animals and hawk feathers. During deer-hunting season they learned to use bows in addition to their rifles, making sure to bless the dead whitetails before gutting, hot blood and steam rising off the snow like a prayer. No doubt my father's nostalgic love for Native American folklore and the Pontiac community in northern Michigan was also perpetuated by watching the culture slowly fade out. Like the time one of his boyhood Pontiac friends fell through the ice on the Manistee River and drowned. Or the local Pontiac man who burned down his own cabin in a drunken rage and then started living in an empty school bus the city gave to him. In my father's youth, even though he was just a boy, it was never as simple as "playing Indian." Without his father around, my dad was comforted not just by his friends but also by a dying culture, its ancient rites of passage disappearing like the last flickering flames of a council fire.

When my parents met, in the early 1970s, my father had experimented with LSD, studied Emerson's transcendentalism, and worked for the State Department of Natural Resources, repairing damaged trout habitats on the Manistee River. Meantime, my mother had joined the "Jesus movement," clothing and feeding the poor of Detroit. Despite their having experienced loss, both remained dedicated to making the best of things, their love for each other a mixture of confused religious aspirations and generational dissociation. They married when my mother was nineteen and my father twenty-one. Living in poverty, they managed to put each other through college, and at one point even lived in a tepee on family land.

When I came into the world my parents had been married five years and were working as caretakers at a juvenile detention center for boys in Lexington, Kentucky, right down the road from Asbury Theological seminary, where my father was studying to be a preacher. Amid the culture of the late 1960s and early 1970s were some who had found a way to blend Jesus with things like rock and roll and beat poetry. My father's long locks and Martin dreadnaught guitar. My mother's flower paintings and braided hair. Dusty Bibles were reread for new meaning. With everyone contributing his own verse, a new breed of transcendental Christian ministers had come out of the woodwork.

My very first years were spent in the detention center hallways, riding on the shoulders of big black boys with names like "Bones" and "Ronny." My parents say I dug my fingers into their afros and pulled and giggled so hard the boys begged my parents to take me.

"You best watch him when he gets older," Bones said to my dad. "Best he not turn out like me, preach."

"God loves you just the way you are, Bones," my dad replied.

Once finished at seminary and the boys' home, my father was appointed to his first parish, which was how my family came to Lydia United Methodist, in a small prairie farming town in rural Minnesota.

Preaching from the pulpit at Lydia, my father would speak openly of his life experience: "The people of the world seem to me like the dying trout habitats we tried to save on the Manistee River when I worked for the DNR in Michigan, which is why I'm in the ministry, standing at this pulpit here in Minnesota. *People* need sanctuary as badly as the dying trout populations." My mother nodded and smiled as my father delivered his sermons.

Inevitably, I heard the same stories over and over again from the wooden pews and at church gatherings in the fellowship hall. At home over dinner, I would hear the finer details of my parents' upbringing, and they would speak about church matters like the dinner table was a war planning room.

"You know, Randy actually shook my hand today after my sermon," my dad said. "I think God is opening his heart."

"Little by little," my mom added. "It comes little by little."

For as confusing as their social, religious ideologies might have been, my parents tried their hardest to guide me sensitively into their hybrid of public and private symbols. I remember the night my father woke me up and took me into the church sanctuary to formally accept Jesus into my heart. I was only six years old.

It was wintertime. I expected snow shoeing together or walking in our winter boots into the dead cornfield behind the parsonage. Instead, I woke to find that he was solemn, kneeling next to my bed and praying with his forehead resting on his folded hands.

"Would you like to accept Jesus into your heart tonight?" He kneeled next to my bed in the moonlight and shadows. His face, cloaked in darkness, looked alien. My body sweated and I felt afraid. I did not understand his question.

"Let's go to the sanctuary," he said.

He walked me through the snowy field between the parsonage and Lydia United Methodist church. He held my hand, and we did not speak to each other. Black-gray clouds drifted like phantoms across the royal blue sky, the stars faint behind the towering light of the full moon.

As he guided me past the dark narthex and into the sanctuary, the furnace rumbled deep below in the loins of the church. I shivered and clenched my father's hand.

"Do you know what it means to ask Jesus into your heart?" my dad asked gently.

"No," I said.

"It means that he lives inside of you and stays there always. He protects you."

"Protects me from the bad guys?" I asked.

"Yes. Always. And from the devil."

I remember the red and black sanctuary. The blood-red carpet. The black shadows. The wooden communion rails. The flickering altar candles. The empty pulpit. The dusty lectern lamp. My father sitting on the edge of the altar. I'm sitting next to him. I'm looking at the carpet. My father's hands are wrapped around mine, holding my hands gently in the prayer position. I repeat the sinner's prayer as he whispers it to me:

> *Dear God. I am a sinner. I ask for your forgiveness. I ask for your son Jesus to come into my heart and save me from my sins. Dear Jesus, thank you for coming into my heart to save me and guide me by the light of your Holy Spirit.*

It is ironic that I was so fearful on the night I accepted Jesus into my heart to atone for my sins, a concept I had little understanding of at six years old. However dark and subtly violent the experience, I remember my excitement. Afterward, my father lay on the red carpet and watched the shadows of the altar on the vaulted ceiling. I lay down next to him, and he held my hand. It was like he owned the place. We had completed some kind of formality. The candles danced and burned brightly. My fear drifted away, and I felt a sense of ownership and entitlement. The sanctuary and church felt brand-new to me, safer and sturdier than before.

Before we left, my father said, "This is for you. Open your hands." He placed a small pewter bear statue in one palm and a small glow-in-the-dark cross in the other. "Keep these by your bed at night, and if you get scared, talk to Jesus or look at the bear for courage. I gave you the bear symbol when you were born. It's a Native

American power animal. Did you know that? It's a very special animal that will help you throughout your life. It will look after you in your dreams. And if you charge that cross under the light of your lamp, it will glow in the dark."

Although I didn't understand the notion of power animals and had no idea of what it meant to accept Jesus into my heart, I received a gift that night; inside the shadowy sanctuary at the altar of Lydia, my father bestowed me with the keys for two seemingly different worlds at once.

CHAPTER 4

LA PURGA

Purging during an ayahuasca ceremony is not like performing normal bodily functions. In holistic health and yoga communities the mind/body connection is emphasized. People meditate to be more present, thinking less and experiencing more, clearing the head of mental detritus. More extreme detoxifying hot yoga classes have become popular all across the United States. Bikram's yoga class, for example, a ninety-minute workout including two sets of twenty-six postures and two breathing exercises in a hundred-plus-degree room, with fifty percent humidity, was designed to detoxify the body and mind. People go to saunas to sweat out holiday debauchery, while ecstatic dance and Pilates awaken the repressed feminine. The list of metaphors and exercise practices related to both psychological and bodily detoxification could go on, but nothing I have experienced comes anywhere close to what it feels like to purge and detoxify the body and mind in an ayahuasca ceremony. Ayahuasca purging is in a league of its own.

When I purge during an ayahuasca ceremony, it is not just the physical release, and it is not just the emotional, spiritual, or psychological release, but the phenomenal combination of all of the above in an astronomically unique event that makes the purge life altering. A scream becomes the unique story of an entire lifetime, reaching out into the periphery of individual freedom and divalike melody. By screaming you reclaim something repressed, fragmented, or forgotten.

The sound of vomiting is inhumanly grotesque, painful, relevant, funny, and finally desperate, until somewhere a mountain crumbles and boulders drop like rain off the side of a cliff centuries old and steeped in words like "karma," and "original sin." Every muscle of the body forces bile and stress out of your soul. And *it's* not just vomit. *It's* everything you've been holding on to for something like the past six years. People releasing baggage like typhoons and avalanches.

At the same time it's not all painful or scary. Laughter during an ayahuasca ceremony is the reunion of thousands of lost children and is often accompanied by tears and sobs like earthquakes, until you laugh so hard you vomit again like the birth of a star. This purge is soul shifting. It is the plate tectonics of your reality. People don't just lose it when they purge. They feel every shred of their existence, of what it really means to be human, until they might burst, and then they explode and survive anyway.

I remember how my very first ayahuasca purge started, evolved, and finally finished my first night at El Puma Negro lodge.

It was raining hard outside the mesa. Thunder boomed over the tops of the trees. Branches snapped and fell as the larger sentinels of the jungle ran for cover, stirring up birds and the sounds of flapping wings in the undergrowth.

The rodent-sized lodge dog, Cucaracha, growled and barked. The vibration of the crickets grew louder and then vanished. Several splashes sounded off one after another, and reptiles disappeared into the brown river. The sound of rain ricocheted off the water.

The *icaro* had changed. The pace of Ethan's melody had quickened. As if Ethan's *icaro* was stirring the soup of a large boiling cauldron, gradually building momentum, the medicine song gathered everybody in the circle into the same vision. Each time the melody dipped into the haunting minor notes, I could feel myself getting sicker.

I saw the mesa sitting inside of a canoe, each one of us lying limp in the hull. It was the same canoe my family had taken out to the lakes during my childhood. The waters were dark and the banks of the river covered in shadows and trees. Red eyes peered at us from the forest. Ethan, who had morphed into a life-sized golden hornet, hovered above the canoe. His translucent wings buzzed at the speed of light. Small sparks of electric white and silver burst off from their tips as he paddled us downriver. Each stroke of Ethan's paddle fell in synch with the rising and falling of the *icaro* melody. Each stroke was also the sound of his *chakapa* leaf rattle, the vague but persistent reminder that I had taken ayahuasca.

As the speed of our journey downriver increased with each paddle stroke, I felt dizzier and dizzier, until I woke in the mesa to find myself on my knees, hovering over my purge bucket in the dark. I choked on stomach acid. My jaw unhinged so wide I thought my eyes might burst. A giant black viper poured out of my mouth. I fell forward as mucus spilled into my bucket.

"Nice healing," Ethan said to me.

His *chakapa* whisked over the top of my head. For a moment I saw the glowing orange of his cigar near my face. Then a cloud of the *mapacho* smoke covered me, and although it was dark I could see the smoke as if it were a glowing, white halo. It smelled sickly sweet. The black viper swam inside the bucket. Ethan's face gyrated in front of mine, half hornet and half human being. Thousands of golden sparks danced around his face.

"How ya feeling?" he asked me.

"I don't know," I said.

I looked down at the bucket to see the black viper was gone. In its place were rainbow strands of light shooting back and forth.

Until that moment I had only read about the purging of an aya-huasca ceremony in books and magazines. I knew the purge could be life-changing, violent, and terrifying. I had read that people could purge addictions and old "stuff," the life baggage each one of us carries, but nothing could have prepared me for it.

Watching my jaw unhinge and a black viper pour out of my mouth, my body clenching like a medieval bone crusher and geysers of unknown substance evacuating my stomach (we had fasted for the entire day before the ceremony, so what was it?), I had sat squarely situated in not just the fear of death by my consummation of aya-huasca but a fear of death so primitive it had simultaneously con-jured the most timeless visions of finality: Hubble-like pictures of dead stars, forest men killing animals and drinking their blood, the underground plates of the earth moving back and forth, the blank stare of a decomposing body, and the nebulous floating void of that which is not physical but always present, that blank container from which all life passes in and out, the place I sat experiencing for the first time as I watched myself purge every last inch of a giant black viper.

Realizing that such little time had passed since I drank my cup of ayahuasca, I wondered if I would make it through to the other side. Could I make it until morning without losing my mind? And if I did lose my mind, would it ever come back?

"We have to learn how to say *yes* to our experiences. Especially if we want to stay centered during an ayahuasca ceremony." Ethan blew smoke over my face again, and I felt the leaves of his *chakapa* rattle brush across my cheeks as another out-of-body vision ensued.

Spouts of flame shot up from the oily muck of a black-red fire swamp. Back in the mesa my body sweated profusely. Each reminder of my body, each droplet of sweat, translated itself into the spouts of flame that shot up from the swamp. Next to the swamp was a stairway that reached from the pits of the bog into a faraway light. Each step upward was painted in silver hieroglyphics, like nothing I had ever seen before. The letters and words on the stairway were more coherent with every ascending step, but the light in the heavens seemed too far away from me.

"I can't do this," I said.

"Believe in yourself," Ethan answered.

"It's too much to expect of someone," I argued.

There was no reply.

I woke in what must have been the ceremonial lodge. It was strangely quiet. The rain was gone. The jungle noises were gone. The *icaro* was gone. Cucaracha was silent. I could not sense Ethan's presence or that of anybody else in the mesa with me. For several moments everything was empty, and then I heard the sounds of one man purging.

I tried to determine which group member was struggling, but I could not trace the sounds back to anybody specific. Whoever the man was, it quickly ceased to matter. He was purging so hard that it was insignificant. He was beyond reach and impaled upon his most arrogant delusions of grandeur; an unseen hand squeezed toxic waste out of him like a wet sponge in the humid jungle grass.

As the man continued to purge, I saw the dragon again (the same dragon that had eaten and regurgitated the old man from my first vision). It wrapped and coiled around the man's chest and throat, but I still could not make out his face. The rainbow-colored serpent squeezed chunks of black matter from the man's stomach into his purge bucket. I saw the man's inner organs. They were pink and red. His veins and arteries and nerve branches glowed and trembled. Each time he vomited, the dragon squeezed its grip tighter and the man's eyeballs jutted farther out of his skull. The purging sounds were so impersonal they were almost beautiful. Almost transcendent. But trying to relax into the sounds, I felt something tugging at my very essence, as if I were a gray puddle pushed by the wind. *Who is that purging?*

Then I cupped my hands over my ears and momentarily saw myself curled into the fetal position, somewhere, disoriented and trying to escape. But escape from what, exactly? Not the effects of the ayahuasca or the visions but something deeper, something residing at my core: the malignant feeling of being insignificant and alone in a universe far too vast and vicious for me to make headway. If it was my responsibility to find happiness, then I would never succeed. Who could?

"I can't do it," I blurted out.

"Yes, you can," Ethan's voice answered.

As if on command from Ethan's voice, I found myself kneeling again in front of my purge bucket. I could feel my body. Thunder clapped above the mesa. Rain pounded the lodge roof so hard I could barely hear Cucaracha howling outside. People were vomiting around me. The medicine song darted through the circle like a jungle snipe. I saw piranhas swimming through the air and devouring demonlike entities as they left people's bodies. The rainbow serpent circled the mesa in the lodge rafters, looking down and watching over us. The guardian creatures were being commanded by Ethan's singing.

Somebody screamed, "I can't do this!"

"It's impossible!" another man yelled.

It became clear to me, as though a black-velvet curtain had been slowly pulled back, that the person I could not see purging in the dark had been each one of us, suffering in exactly the same way. The man I had not been able to identify in the darkness was not anybody in particular but rather the entire mesa. The illusion of absolute individuality was exposed. It was as if all of the existentialist philosophers I had read and loved had instantly become people no different from me, revealing suffering for what it often is: a collective state of being, something we each feel despite our stories and reasons, not because of them.

"We can all walk toward the light," Ethan said. "One moment at a time. We make it through the night by focusing our minds and believing in ourselves and each other."

"I don't believe in myself," I said. My words choked in my throat as another stream of vomit left my mouth. "I don't believe in any of you, either. I'm sorry." I pounded my fists on the floor of the mesa. "I'm a tourist; I admit it. Please make this stop!"

"Don't exaggerate. Life gets easier when you stop lying to yourself. It took courage for you to drink ayahuasca," Ethan said. "And you're being honest right now, not cowardly. This is *your* moment. Right now, *you* are becoming a man. You wanted to drink ayahuasca. This is what ayahuasca medicine is about. It's about getting real."

I vomited once more. I could see myself changing before my eyes. I saw visions of myself as an adult, calmer and more reflective. What did I know, anyway? I was experiencing something so far out of the ordinary, so transcending of my everyday boundaries, what could I possibly claim to know with absolute certainty? Knowing I would never be the same again, and knowing I could never capture the profundity of what was taking place in the mesa, I knew that I would become a kinder and more humble person. I would not become kinder because the ayahuasca was imparting a moral lesson but rather because there would be no other choice. I would have to admit, from that moment forward, that I didn't have the slightest grasp on anything. My only truth would be the simplest statements: I'm breathing, and my heart is beating. I'm alive.

o————————o

Ethan sat in his rocking chair, collected and professional. "That last *icaro* melody was Domingo's," he said. "And it was taught to him by Arturo. They taught me the *icaro* during my apprenticeship. So that was an official medicine-song greeting from my teachers. They hope they can meet you the next time you visit El Puma Negro."

"Next time?" a woman asked.

"Of course," Ethan joked. "You'll be ready to do this all over again by tomorrow afternoon!"

The woman vomited and then began to laugh.

"I had no idea something like this was even possible," I said.

In the brief moments of clarity that followed my first round of purging, I reflected on the difficulty of explaining ayahuasca to empirically minded, "scientific" people. I thought specifically of my best friend back in the United States, a Ph.D. chemistry student and intern at NASA's Jet Propulsion Laboratory. Before I had left for Peru he had said to me, "You know your brain can produce some pretty amazing things. That doesn't mean you're going to be entering the spirit world."

As I briefly thought of my friend I felt an overwhelming sense of love for him. I imagined hearing his commentary next to me in the mesa and knew that he would probably not be able to rely on his empirical reductionism to quite the same extent. Even if my brain had been firing randomly and creating the spirit world I had entered, even if it could all be reduced to some "thing," then what chance occurrence of reality had created creatures so puzzled by their own existence? And how had ancient human beings discovered this unusual drink? And how had they passed down the exact recipe for hundreds, maybe thousands, of years?

But the more I pondered in the mesa, the more my philosophical questions and answers became nothing more than another self-made virus, the equivalent of pulling my own hair on the mesa floor, pounding my fists until I would purge again with the help of a gringo shaman and the rainbow-colored dragon.

"I had absolutely no clue about any of this," I said.

"Of course not," Ethan replied. "You can't know until you find out."

"You drank a full cup, didn't you?"

"That's right," he answered.

"How did you learn to lead these ceremonies?"

"With good teachers and a lot of hard work," he said.

Throughout the course of nearly five years, Ethan had lived and trained in the jungle: fishing for his food in the Amazon River, bathing with natives, collecting and harvesting his own plants and healing herbs, and learning the medicine path from his maestros.

After hundreds of ceremonies and dozens of rigorous plant diets in training, Ethan had earned the title of practitioner only months before I had arrived in the Amazon. Arturo and Domingo had given him full responsibility for the mesa and had instructed him to perform ceremonies alone for the time being. From the first day Ethan had begun studying, whenever locals asked Domingo and Arturo about training a white man, they would say, "We've seen that he has a good heart, and we've received the vision to train him correctly.

The ayahuasca medicine vine was first given to the people of the forest as a gift from the one who planted the garden. It was given to the people for healing, and it should be given to the rest of the world in the same way. Let fall on us what will. We are going to train this man to be a master ayahuasca shaman."

It was only the midpoint of my first ayahuasca ceremony. While the rain softened, each of us in the mesa enjoyed a small break: the sounds of shared laughter and the feeling of our body on the solid earth. Ethan was quiet in his rocking chair, rocking back and forth in the dark, whistling lightly under his breath, and puffing a mystical *mapacho* cigar.

CHAPTER 5

ACHRA/ARACHNA-PHOBIA

Some of our earliest fears stay with us the longest. As children our identity structures are vast. In the womb we live in the amniotic fluid where the separation between our bodies and our mother's body is indistinguishable. We are one.

When we come out of the womb we experience our first limitation. We are strangled out of our mother's uterus. We travel down a dark tunnel. There is a bright light at the end. Our mother is screaming from the pain of separation. When we emerge from the birth canal our mother relaxes, and then *we* are the ones to scream as we breathe on our own for the first time, eyes blinded by the light.

As little babies our consciousness is oceanic. We cannot tell the world apart from our own fingers. Then we grow older and develop a sense of self and a self-structure. The structure expands safely as we grow by the guidance of our mother and father, our family, our tribe, nature, and community. When it doesn't work this way, people can become sick. Instead of sharing intimacy, we can harm each other. When victimization takes place, especially when we are young or defenseless, toxic identity structures manifest. If we don't have the proper healers and healing rituals we become chronically dis-eased.

Ayahuasca medicine is about facing fear and healing unhealthy self-identification structures put in place by damaging relationships, poor choices, and victimization events from all stages of life, especially those occurring when the person was relatively defenseless.

When you see your fears in an ayahuasca ceremony and react to them, you purge. You will laugh or cry or vomit or defecate, or your muscles might loosen up, or you might yawn louder than ever before or burp or moan. When the purge is over your everyday reaction to the same fear will be different because your boundaries are different. Little by little, you learn to see all your fears the same and sit upright during ceremonies, facing more intense levels of *the one fear* without overreacting. In place of overreaction you will release into your peace of mind by simple instinct, just like athletes use pure muscle memory at high levels of performance.

Ayahuasca teaches us how to instinctively release fear, in every moment of every day, as a constant and always evolving discipline. Ayahuasca teaches us that fear is not an opponent and that life itself is an ally.

Some of my oldest fear was strangely wrapped like hieroglyphics around traumatizing events from my childhood. For many ceremonies my fear showed up in the form of spiders and heights. Slowly during ceremonies I peeled away the layers of my fear and saw how these symbols were given their power. I saw the *same fear* behind each particular disguise.

When I was a little boy, on occasion, I stayed with my grandmother in Michigan during the summer so my parents could lead church mission trips. My grandmother and I ate popcorn and watched *The Golden Girls* and *Cheers* on television. We pieced puzzles together on her sewing table and went to the beach in Lake City. Every day we walked down the dirt road to the mailbox, which had a painted image of a rabbit and her last name, my mother's maiden name: Hasenauer. My grandmother explained to me that the Hasenauer family seal has a rabbit in the center, and she explained to me that I was partly German, Swedish, and Irish. She told me not to let my father's dad tell me I was only Dutch.

"Your mother's side of the family is where you get your good genes from," she said.

At some point my grandmother introduced me to a next-door neighbor's boy, Jason. He and I played together in the woods and red-fern fields behind my grandmother's Michigan cottage almost every day that summer. He was much older than I. I was six years old. He was twelve.

"It's good for you to play with an older boy. Jason is more rambunctious. Your mother babies you too much. Protestants are like that. We are going to teach you the Catholic work ethic." My grandmother stood next to me at the dining room table one afternoon, teaching me how to strike a match and light a candle.

"Hold on to it now. Don't be so afraid, or it will burn you."

I dropped the candle onto the table and looked at my grandmother in fear.

"Give me your fingers and be a big boy," she said. This time she lit the match and tried to help me light the candle, her hand holding mine like a steel vice.

"I'm afraid," I said. I started to squirm.

"Then you'll get burned," she replied. She held me tighter and wouldn't let me go.

As I danced up and down trying to squirm away, she squeezed me and waited until the match came down to my fingers. When the fire burned me I yelped. She blew out the candle.

"You can't be afraid," she said angrily. "Not if you're going to light a candle."

My face filled with tears, and I ran through the kitchen and to the basement to get away from my grandmother, sucking on my singed finger as I went. At the top of the long stairs to the basement I felt woozy. The stairs seemed higher than a mountain. I felt that I was too far up, and I was dizzy, afraid I might fall.

One night later that same summer, instead of watching *The Golden Girls* and *Cheers*, Jason came for a slumber party. We were together in the same bed in the guestroom and stayed up late playing with our flashlights. The television buzzed gently in the living room, and my grandmother laughed occasionally from down the hallway.

"Let's play boyfriend and girlfriend," he said. "Take off your clothes."

He took off his clothes. I could feel his naked body next to mine. Then I took off my pajamas and lay naked next to him.

"Come under here," he said.

I crawled underneath the sheets and felt his warm body soft against mine.

"Now kiss me down there," he said.

I kissed his penis with a soft peck, the same way my mother kissed me at bed every night and the way my grandmother kissed my forehead when she said hello or good-bye.

"No, not like that, stupid," he said. "Like this. Lay down." Then he sucked on me the way you would suck a Popsicle. Strange tingling sensations flooded my body. They felt overwhelming and new.

"See. Feels good, doesn't it? Now you do it to me. Except you have to do it until I say stop. Don't stop until I say it's time to stop."

I remember doing it. Then I remember it tasted salty. It felt alive inside of my mouth, like a lazy snake. Then I heard my grandmother's footsteps pad down the hallway. Jason slapped me on the back of my head. It stung sharp from the back of my skull to my forehead.

"Stop it, stupid, your grandma is coming. She can't see us doing this."

"Doing what?"

"You really are dumb." He scurried to put his pajamas on, and while I did the same my grandmother called to me.

"You boys need to sleep if Jason is going to stay the night."

Jason looked at me like a wild animal. All at once he became like a snarling beast. His whole body shook. "If you say a *word* . . ." he said, "I will break your arm." He jammed his finger on my forehead and grabbed my left arm tightly, all the way down to the bone.

Panic swept through my body, mingling with the first sexual sensations I'd ever experienced. I felt sick.

As I lay trembling I watched a spider on the ceiling above my head. It sat crouched in the corner, hanging upside down. I stared at the spider, watching its long legs, its secret eyes, its hidden fangs, its mysterious thoughts, petrified of what would happen to me next, hearing Jason whisper, "I will break your arm if you tell anybody," over and over again.

He forced me into similar situations with the same threat for the rest of my stay that summer, grabbing my left arm whenever my grandmother wasn't around, and always saying, "I will break your arm if you tell anybody."

In many ancient shamanic and tribal traditions, when human beings developed self-identity it was important for them to remember their greater identity in the source energy of the universe, that which has most traditionally been called God, or the Great Spirit, the *One*, or Love. In order to function in the greater world of nature and the tribe, a young man or woman was taken through an initiation ritual or rite of passage. The ritual gave young men and women an experiential reminder of the fact that all life is eternal.

Women were taught the eternal nature of life by witnessing first-hand the turnover in their bodies. Following the moon and watching their eggs birth, blossom, and shed with the release of blood and the uterine lining. Fertility rites were essential for women. The visionary teaching device was a woman's very own physiology. Men, on the other hand, were taught the same lesson by attending their first hunt and experiencing the nature of death. Additionally, men were often taken from the coddling of their mother and left in a cave or hole in the ground.

The young man would remain under shamanic supervision while he fasted and stayed awake for many days in the dark, waiting until a visionary experience took place to emerge into the light. When the man emerged from the cave or dark hole (a symbolic womb), he was carefully nursed back to health by his elders and the tribal medicine man. Like the women and their menstrual cycle, the young man would be in touch with a greater sense of life because of his near-death experience. He might even be given a cut on his thigh to represent the earning of his own womb. These coming-of-age rituals taught people the nature of life, death, and eternity.

In a sense, vision quests are happening all the time. If we are not taught how to face fear through rites of passage, by our elders, by ceremonies, or by guiding hands, then we are skirting our social responsibility, and future generations will be missing the proper tools to face fear when it comes, from the wilderness, the job, a romantic relationship, the street, the government, or from people who try to take something from us that doesn't belong to them. Without knowing how to face fear, we cannot heal. The two things are the same.

At sixteen years old I was a junior camp counselor at a Christian Bible camp for children where I spent the summer teaching little kids about the performing arts. That was my area of expertise because I was in the drama club at my high school.

On the last night of camp, after the boys' giggling stopped and the flashlights were extinguished, I lay awake on my back looking out the cabin window at the stars. I heard the sounds of a loon calling on the lake. The young boys snored peacefully. A bullfrog croaked in a sick rhythm near the shoreline. The moon shone brightly. Stars covered the sky.

I drifted in and out of sleep. I dreamed still partially awake and hypnagogic. My dream was the replay of a memory from childhood.

"They won't move. Just watch 'em. They'll sit there until they die!"

A fat boy named Carter, who is called Killowats at school, is showing me how to kill a toad in his backyard. It's a Sunday afternoon in August, and the stench of a neighboring pig farm is wafting through the rural Minnesota air. We're standing next to a rusty orange and black fire pit in Killowats's backyard. He has set a handful of tree toads into the fire pit. The sunlight is beating down on the toads. It's over one hundred degrees. I'm wiping the sweat off my dirty forehead.

"Why do you want them to die?" I ask. "You like to kill innocent animals or what?" But Killowats won't answer me. Instead he grunts and kicks the side of the fire pit with his filthy tennis shoes. "Why are you so angry?" I asked.

Although I cannot clearly remember our actual childhood exchange, in my dream he spoke to me with just his eyes and the angry look on his face, saying, "Your parents made you play with me because your father is the pastor of the church and my mom is the new church secretary. We don't have as much money as your family does, and your family probably just pities us. So does the church. You don't even like me. And you can't tell me what to do. I'm not afraid of you. I'm not afraid of anything. Look at those toads. They don't move when they're dying. They're not scared of anything. But you are!"

Then I felt a sting in my body and woke from my sleep. I sat up in my cabin bed sweating and severely nauseous. I went to the outhouse and vomited. Twenty-four hours later I returned home from my summer camp job and collapsed on the staircase to my basement bedroom while carrying my duffel bag. At the top of the stairs I had become dizzy and I fainted.

Within twenty-four hours a small red bite on my arm had risen to the size of a golf ball. A red streak of blood underneath my skin had traveled from the lump on my left forearm all the way up to my biceps. An intense fever had swept over my body in only minutes before I collapsed.

I remember my last moments of consciousness in the stairwell perfectly. Everything slowed down. I looked at the white ceiling and saw every detail exactly, the little grains, the waves, the particles. I felt afraid and almost panicked, but then as I felt myself slipping away, I thought, *I remember* this.

I woke in a pale white emergency room with a doctor holding a small photo of a fat brown spider in front of my face.

"It's a brown recluse," he said.

I was groggy and realized the doctor was talking to me, but I didn't know how long it had been. "They sometimes nest in those cabins up North," he said. "That's one of the dangers of being a camp counselor out in the woods like that. He must have got you in your sleep. You're lucky that streak of red right there didn't make it to your heart. That's blood poisoning. Your heart would have pumped the venom throughout your whole body, and that would have been it."

Next to my hospital bed was a small dish filled with yellow puss and brown water and red blood. The doctor and emergency room nurse had lanced the golf-ball-sized ulcer on my left arm and injected it with antivenom. I couldn't remember any of it.

The spider venom had entered my bloodstream through my left arm during my strange dream about the toads and Killowats. Almost like falling asleep, almost like a dream, I would have left this world and my body the same way I came into it: without memory or narrative, with simple and profound sensations, everything slowed down, everything on its own terms, returning out through a dark tunnel and toward a white ceiling of light.

When I came home from the emergency room I climbed out the second-story window of the parsonage and scampered onto the roof. I brought my journal and sat down to write. I wrote about my dream from the last night of camp about Killowats and about my fear of spiders. I looked at my left arm over and over again in the moonlight, examining the fading streak of red blood underneath my skin.

I had always feared heights. But sitting on the roof I felt changed. Everything was kinder and simpler. I could see through to the other side of the veil. It wasn't a big deal. In fact it was simple. In my journal I wrote: *It has never been heights or spiders that scare me. It's that I'm afraid I will lose control. Afraid I might die before I'm ready. Something will get me that I can't see coming.*

While I sat on the edge of the parsonage rooftop, I gazed at the steeple of my father's Methodist church down the street. The glowing cross perched on the top of the steeple. It was lit up orange-red on white, the ancient executioner's block engulfed in the symbolic alchemical flames of the Holy Spirit.

I wrote: *Maybe that's what the cross was all about? Maybe it had nothing to do with sin. Maybe Jesus wanted to show people not to be afraid of death? But, if life is eternal, then I need to find the real Christianity. I need to find a better church because I think my dad is losing his faith. . . .*

Then my father's voice called me from the house. He was leaning outside the first-story window, his face hidden in the shadows of night.

He called up to me, "You're just back from the hospital, son. You need to come inside. It's not safe up there."

His voice sounded far away and sad, like he was doing his duty as a father, but at the same time a tucked-away part of him envied my youthful spirit. He seemed to mourn his giant suburban church outside Minneapolis. He seemed stumped by the fast ascension of his career as a Methodist pastor. How far he had come since his first parish at Lydia United Methodist, yet how distant he was from our family.

"What were you writing about in your journal up there?" he asked me.

"Nothing," I said.

The truth was that by the time I was sixteen my father had written about most everything in his sermons already. I felt there was no room for him to take a serious interest in my original thoughts, as if he hadn't already communicated to all his different congregations everything there was to know. In his attempts to relate to me, he had a way of responding to my most original thoughts in his pastoral tone, speaking like a theologian and then segueing into his sad cadence when he failed to connect with me, like he was guilty of something or like he was looking for himself in his own voice, searching for the secret chord.

CHAPTER 6

·———·

BEING OF ONE MIND

As the rain let up and storm clouds rumbled away into the distance and the jungle dripped dry, the animals and insects chirped. I couldn't feel my body or my face. Again I was weightless and wandering among the *coo-ree, coo-ree* of loud birds in the bushes.

I saw the phantom faces of parrots, electric blue and green, hanging upside down and right side up from the trees. Long beaks. Glowing eyes. *Coo-ree, coo-ree.* Silver panthers sleeked through the shadows, while golden fawns lay in the green ferns. Pink, white caiman alligators swam through the air with sharp teeth and fast tails.

One of the men sitting next to me said, "This is incredible. Can you believe this is happening?"

"I believe *everything* at this point," I said. Everybody in the mesa laughed.

"Why do apprenticeships even matter?" The man sitting next to me could not comprehend the need for shamanic help. "Everything

43

is one. Nobody knows shit about shit. Why do you need a shaman to guide you? It's silly. We're all shamans."

The self-righteousness of the man's statement sent a small shockwave through the mesa. I felt sick to my stomach. Somebody else said a disbelieving "Wow," as if what he meant was "You've got some nerve, pal." Someone else farted and then dry heaved. Ethan said nothing. His *mapacho* cigar glowed orange and then black as he puffed from his rocking chair.

Then it was quiet again in the lodge. Cucaracha snored like a small barometer for the psychic intensity of the ceremony. Outside in the jungle, the cicadas came to life in a musical wave band. I heard the stacked layers of harmonic resonance that comprised thousands upon thousands of crickets.

I used to hear crickets like this when I was a kid, I thought to myself. *I think my hearing was better back then.*

The different sounds reflected back at me like prisms, like science class, a wave-patterned movement of colors matching the frequencies of the cicada, both rhythmically and acoustically, a geometric flowing spectrum, like the waves of the ocean or quickly moving clouds in high-speed photography. Within the cloud thousands of colors all matched and dazzled and morphed into each other like the most spectacularly sequenced fireworks display, each note and pitch, each cicada group represented by a color and a wave, the single crickets firing off as single light particles. The colors were red, orange, yellow, blue, indigo, and violet, changing shades and spilling into each other to create hues and tones like the palette of a painter.

"Who knew crickets were so incredible?" I asked. Everybody in the mesa laughed and giggled again. Someone yawned.

"Ayahuasca is so cool," somebody else said.

"Life is so cool," somebody echoed.

"We are all in ONE body," Ethan said sharply.

Although his statement was clearly esoteric, the suddenness of his remark was particularly mysterious. Like Ethan was tipping us off to something happening in the mesa.

"One body," Ethan repeated quietly.

I sat up on my mattress.

"Have we been talking aloud?" I asked.

Ethan chuckled.

Other people around the mesa sat up on their mattresses, too.

"Wait, who said, 'Why do apprenticeships even matter?'" somebody asked.

"I did," the man next to me admitted. "Pretty loudly, I guess!"

"You did say that, right?"

"Well, I *thought* it," the man answered.

"Holy shit," someone said. "We were speaking *telepathically!*"

"Adam was talking about the crickets," a woman said. "That got us laughing."

"But we laughed out loud," I said. "I know we laughed out loud, right?"

"So how did we hear each other thinking, exactly?" another person chimed in.

"Ayahuasca opens up the channels and makes psychic communication possible," Ethan said. "We always share in the experience of life. Life is never in a vacuum, and your thoughts are *never* separate from actions. *You* are never separate from your body, from the sounds you make, or from the way you move. You can hear each other clearly during a ceremony because everything has been opened."

I realized for the first time the fluidity of time and space. Not as a concept but by way of having a telepathic human experience that was beyond a shadow of a doubt, nonnegotiable, sitting in front of my face. Telepathy was real to me. It was no longer a hokey concept or a book on the new age shelf or the crazy gothic girl at the boy-girl party from junior high school.

"Everybody should try this stuff at least once," I said.

Ethan responded quickly in a stern and teacherly voice, "Ayahuasca is a medicine, Adam. It's not 'stuff.' These ceremonies are not about tripping out or toying around. Even though we have fun together, we shouldn't be disrespectful."

I lay on my back contemplating the word "stuff." It was quiet.

Outside the mesa windows the sky flashed lightning in the distance. The darkest part of the night was past, and the light purple of four a.m. shone brightly, like a radiant jewel. The jungle dripped. The storm was gone. The cicadas, birds, bullfrogs, and insects simmered to a light buzz. I felt my body again. Like waking to find my legs asleep in the night, I sensed my physical presence as a heavy weight, a dull mass accompanied by small reminders of my physical ending points, things like joints and shoulders and knees. I sighed deeply, still pondering the word "stuff."

Ethan whistled a soft *icaro*, and, as though my soul could not help but follow the melody, my body faded again. This time the speed at which my vision began was slower. The vision itself was softer and not without sensations in my fingers, the air in my lungs, and my cheek resting on the damp mattress. The purple color of the four a.m. sky still hung somewhere on the periphery of my consciousness, reminding me time was passing.

"This *stuff*," I mumbled. "This *stuff*."

Then I cried and then choked on my tears. My arms and legs trembled.

o———————o

Fire raged from the World Trade Center towers and people walked lifelessly on the city streets. Suitcase bombs exploded in the empty subways. The stock market was empty on Wall Street. Dollars floating in the air. People walked like zombies in shopping malls, hardly recognizing each other, passing by with little desire to do anything but shop for more, and more, and to be left alone, unconscious of the destruction and flames surrounding them. Fat people wiped grease from their mouths and little children sat glued in front of television sets.

Waste rolled into thousands of toilet bowls lining the outside of an empty football stadium. Children hurled their video game controllers at the wall. Losing. Angry fists. And husbands shotgunned beers and beat women. I saw horror films and 3-D glasses. Broken down zoos and artificial food in boxes.

Then I saw myself. How lost my family had become. How quickly things had gone wrong for everybody. How alone I had felt and how desperate I was for an answer. Becoming a fundamentalist. The incessant evangelism. And then the drugs. The lines of powder snorted off mirrors. OxyContin, morphine, Vicodin. The cases of alcohol. Gin every night, by myself. The cartons of cigarettes. Smoking a pack every day. Panic attacks alone in my bathroom. The voices in my head. The packages of condoms. The women coming and going like blinking traffic lights. Being afraid of commitment. The dark church sanctuary. My mother and father fighting. My father's nervous breakdown. My father and grandfather yelling at each other. All of the secrets and lies. My refrigerator filled with disgusting food. Lying to myself. Lying to myself. Over and over. Cartons of curdled milk filled with hormones. My nourishment, canned and frozen, wilted. Nothing fresh. And then, finally, the jungle coming at me like a freight train, buzzing and breathing like a living beast.

I woke in the mesa, stumbling toward the windows at the back of the lodge, grasping at the trees in the night, trying to run myself into the mouth of the forest. Cucaracha yipped. Ethan was quick behind me and sat me down in a hammock that hung from the rafters near the lodge kitchen.

"You can't dwell on gloom and doom," Ethan said to me.

"But everything is going to hell," I said. "Can't you see? Human beings are a virus. The United States is spiritually dead. I've read about the Mayan prophecies. Twenty twelve is coming!"

"The universe is always balanced," Ethan answered. "It's talking to you right now if you'll listen. Things might not be fair between human beings, but they are always fair between human beings and God. You need to be careful what you fill your head with. There is no such thing as *stuff*."

"I'm going to be sick," I said. "I've told people they were going to hell if they didn't become Christian. I threw my life away. Our world is going to hell. We're all sinners," I said. "Not even aya-huasca can save us. It's too late!"

"We are all good people at the core. We are not sinners. That's a lie," Ethan said.

"No it's not," I answered, still watching hellish visions pass before my eyes. "You're the one *lying*."

Ethan walked across the lodge nonchalantly and picked up a purge bucket from the mesa floor. Before he could give me the bucket I fell forward from the hammock and vomited onto the floorboards. A million racing images left my mouth.

"I really want this to be over," I said. I was standing next to Ethan, bent over. It was getting lighter in the mesa. "I'm never doing this again," I added.

"Why don't you take a shower," he said.

"Am I okay to take a shower?"

"Of course you are."

"Yeah. You're right," I said. "I can do this. The water will help me."

A feeling of optimism had returned after purging, though I could feel the lingering presence of the ayahuasca vision world still moving all around me. I walked to the gravity shower at the back of the lodge, sober enough to make my way around for the first time. Brand-new thoughts filled my head. *Who could I ever be but myself? Even when I'm trying to be something else, it's still me doing the struggling, isn't it? I don't have to struggle so much. Against what, anyway? I've only been struggling against myself.*

Unconsciously, I had opened the shower faucet. When the cold river water from the shower nozzle needled into my naked body I shook like I was being electrocuted. The shock forced me to my knees at the bottom of the shower basin. I found myself knee deep in water, surrounded as far as my eyes could see by rows of Greek pillars reaching skyward like Babylonian towers. Blazing stars hung in the deep space above my head. Comets whistled through the dark. Thousands of light particles fell from the heavens, synched up with the water from the shower nozzle, grazing my head and fingers, resting and dissolving on the surface of the murky water, which was actually the tiles of the shower floor. I shivered as I came in and out of my body.

"Remember to focus your mind and always walk your talk," Ethan's voice called to me from the mesa at the other end of the lodge, as if announcing a final test for the night.

My head became heavy again, and my thoughts self-righteous: *From this moment forward I will be a committed disciple of the ayahuasca medicine path. I will learn to focus my mind. I could become an incredible master shaman, even better than Ethan, and I could change the world. I could lead a religious revolution. The second coming . . .*

In the distance, walking on water, I saw Him.

CHAPTER 7

SHAPE SHIFTING

The traditional role of a shaman or medicine man is ambiguous because the position of the shaman is not a stable one. The shaman is a shape shifter. Accordingly, shamanic talent lies in the ability to address multiple needs and navigate multiple dimensions of consciousness at the same time. A shaman will intuit archetypes and patterns within the worlds of the personal, societal, and the universal (perhaps all at once) and then relay his findings to others as a form of instruction, ritual, healing, work of art, song, or ceremony.

In order to perform teachings and healings a shaman generally undergoes an initiation experience that breaks open his boundaries between these personal, societal, and universal layers of existence. The history of shamanism demonstrates that most shamans suffer tragedy, loss, sickness, fear, or a near death experience at some point during their initiation, most often unexpectedly in childhood or young adulthood. The difference between a traditional shaman and a layperson is that a shaman can lead others safely through psychic crisis or has received the vision of a structured ritual to be used for healing.

In past times a shaman's sense of self could be so foreign to a tribe or community that a separate tepee or village was erected solely for the medicine people. Shamans are sometimes aloof and hermetic figures who interact less with the tribe and more with solitude and nature. Given their psychic initiation, shamans do not need to identify themselves as just one type of being. As a result shamans can bring balance and harmony to the diversity of dimensions within other life-forms: humans, animals, ecosystems, concepts, pathologies, and so forth. Through the initiation and training process, a shaman learns to manipulate the structures of energy/spirit to create new life. A shaman is a self-regenerator. A shaman makes things new. This is why shamans can heal people. Shamans lead people safely through psychic or spiritual death and into a new form or self-identity.

For example, a shaman might be someone like a young girl who encounters a jaguar in the forest quite naturally one day while gathering fruit. The cat mauls the girl, and the girl falls into a coma for several weeks. When the girl returns miraculously to life, she recounts the experience of what happened to her when she was mauled by the cat. Like the common "near death" stories that have been told for centuries in books, the young girl has an experience of her self as many new and different things. We might imagine the girl sitting next to the tribal fire, wild eyed, explaining her vision to the elders.

"First I saw myself becoming a panther," she says. "The jaguar was eating me. I became the cat. Then I left my body, and I was like the wind. Then I was the night sky. Then I was the waters. Then fire. Then a great hand placed me back onto the ground of our tribe. I spoke to dead people. I spoke to the eagle and then to mother earth. She told me secret things about the web of life."

When the girl comes back from the coma her consciousness no longer experiences itself as merely human. Instead the girl sees herself as a future adult already, possessing something ageless called a soul. She sees herself having died and having been born all over again. She feels her life force connected to the greater spirit of the planet. She understands animals differently, and she has an understanding, not an idea, of the Great Spirit and web of life.

"Why are you so sad? You used to play with us," says one of the little girl's friends.

The young shamaness sees that the other girls do not yet know of their many faces. She therefore cannot play with the others the way she used to because she cannot enter their reality without bearing the awkward signs of her initiation, which only confuse and scare the other girls.

Walking through the forest alone the young shamaness looks at the trees and rivers; she no longer sees inanimate material, and she no longer places a conceptual scale of value between herself and the animals the way she used to. Instead she sees many patterns and relationships she never saw before. She begins to intuit the functions and patterns of her tribe, of her body, and of the buffalo and bird migrations. She understands the ecological role of the eagle and owl and the changing of the seasons, the meanings of the moon and stars.

The tribal shaman responds to the young shaman initiate around the evening fire, recognizing his new apprentice.

"The Great Spirit has given you counsel. This is important. You must live near my tepee and learn all that I have in my medicine bag [the insights, rituals, and tools the shaman has learned since his initiation]. Spirit will soon test your powers," he says.

As the girl grows with the guidance of the tribal healer she learns to fight the desire to use her ability for selfish gain. She learns to use shamanic practitioner tools in order to use her psychic powers constructively. Just because she has survived a psychic initiation does not necessarily mean that she will use her talents for good. If she is not trained she could become a witch doctor, a *bruja*, or a sorcerer.

Understanding the dark side of shamanism is important. Often people like to believe that all indigenous cultures were unanimously friendlier, more down to earth, more harmonious, wiser, and more spiritual than our contemporary Western paradigm. This couldn't be further from the truth. While the history of shamanism is replete with many good insights, traditions, and wisdom, shamanism also has played a dark role in things like tribal politics, warfare, and social disputes. Just as readily as ayahuasca, for example, might be used to heal a patient, a shaman could also use ayahuasca to cast psychic attack spells on neighboring tribes, throw hexes at competing shamans, hypnotize, or take money from jealous wives or lustful young men to use love incantations on unsuspecting victims.

Because the power of visualization is so strong and the psychic connections to other life-forms so fluid during an ayahuasca ceremony, a shaman can cast spells just by sending negative thoughts at someone while in the visionary space. When a shaman's lust for power influences his abilities, a shaman can easily allow his talent to be used for destruction rather than creation. Visionary ability does not always make someone a healer, and a visionary plant does not always make "medicine."

Translating the historical dark side of shamanism to the contemporary world is not hard. Scientists who see into the nature of the universe can use their wisdom to create better energy resources for the world, or they can allow their desire for money, fame, or power to influence their work, creating the next suitcase-sized nuclear bomb. Similarly, any religionists who see into the heart of humanity can use their vision to justify conquest or peacemaking alike. Vision itself is not enough. It is what we do with a vision that matters. For this reason, traditional healers and what we might call "good shamans" create rituals meant to promote peace and vitality among all beings. Even then, a "good shaman" does not mean "better person," and a good shaman should not be made into an object of worship. For this reason, shamans are often referred to as doctors, healers, or even "road men" guiding the way or getting us back on track. Once we are back on track, a shaman encourages us to learn to heal ourselves in the future. A good shaman also hopes we might learn to heal each other. A good shaman knows that each one of us is a shaman.

Some of the most common practitioner tools of the healer shaman are, and were, plants and plant remedies, musical instruments, symbolic art, and storytelling. A shaman might prescribe a particular plant to heal a particular type of illness (whether it be physical or psychological). Musical instruments and song might be used to induce hours of trance, the trance entraining the sick patient in a psychic lesson of some kind and the rhythmic sounds and melodies invoking a particular brain wave meant to reset the body's biorhythm to homeostasis again.

Similarly, art could be displayed or taught as a form of therapy and teaching. Even storytelling and myth-making will communicate the deeper metaphors of the psyche, tribe, and greater universe. Regardless of what tool is used, the work of a shaman is not purely magical. In other words, although shamanism is commonly thought of as mystical, it might better be called misunderstood. There is a profound level of technique and structure shamans must learn and create in order to perform their duties safely. It's not just mysticism and magic. They must learn teaching and healing on three levels: the personal, the societal, and the universal.

On *the personal level*, the shaman will use a combination of intuition and knowledge of structures/archetypes within the psyche and nature in order to perform healings. For example, the healing properties of certain plants will be understood by experimentation. A shaman might meditate in the forest among the plants until he understands a visionary interpretation of a specific plant's role in the ecology. Once the ecology of a particular plant is intuited, its archetypal pattern can be placed over the identical structure within the human psyche to reach a diagnosis.

Next a shaman might ingest the plant remedy in his diet until he established a working relationship with the plant itself. By doing this, the shaman connects with the life force of the prescribed plant medicine, its spirit. The shamanic administration of medicine is then a matter of relational holistic healing. The plant remedy is both a prescription and a mediation, or fusion dialogue between life-forms.

To continue the example, let's imagine that a tribe member is extremely accident-prone. She is constantly running into unfortunate situations. One night while standing under the stars, the young woman says to the shaman, "I feel I have bad luck. Bad things keep happening to me unexpectedly. Can you help me?"

The shaman might meditate upon his knowledge of the plants until he matches an affinity. He remembers the earlike receiver plant that perches on the tops of the trees above the jungle canopy, like insect antennae gathering periphery information. He intuits a match between the plant's physical position in nature and the lack of peripheral vision the accident-prone woman has in her psyche. The shaman tests the healing theory by building a relationship with the plant through ingestion, or smoking, or taking its sap. Upon ingestion he sees that his psychic reception increased and then confirms the prescription for his patient. After ingesting the plant regularly with the shaman in private ceremonies, the young woman finds herself avoiding a mud slide on her walk home from the river. She thanks the shaman.

"The medicine spirits of the plant and your guidance helped me today. I am clean from my sickness. I feel alert again."

"I give thanks back to the plants and to the spirit of the one who planted them," he replies.

On *the societal level*, a shaman might spend time meditating with and observing the deer.

"The deer spirit is not a match for our hunt any longer," he says at the tribal council.

By watching the deer one afternoon in a trance, he intuits that the deer are sick and thus informs the tribe that sickness in some of the people is a result of eating diseased deer. Then the shaman might observe overpopulation in the rabbits and suggest hunting rabbits for the time being, always sure to keep a balance.

Finally, on *the universal level*, the shaman might counsel a man grieving the loss of his wife by addressing the personal, societal, and ecological dimensions of consciousness all at once. Let's imagine the man cannot stop grieving beyond the set time the tribe allows. In the meantime the tribe is also upset because the shaman will not let the tribe use the nearest watering hole, because it will interfere with the beaver population.

The man's grieving will not stop, and he is plagued by depression. The already frustrated tribe wants the man to release the spirit of his wife and stop spreading his sadness around. So the shaman reflects both upon the man and the tribe's situations. He sees the way in which the tribe had interfered with the beavers' homes at the nearby watering hole and intuits the way that greed can damage greater networks. He sees the same presence in the man who lusts after his wife's ghost as if she was his possession.

The shaman then tells the grieving man to go to the watering hole and sit for five days inside a stone circle without sleep or water. While the grieving man sits near the watering hole at the edge of the beaver dam he passes into a visionary state of consciousness during which he is reminded of his greater relationship to nature. He is reminded of the coming and going of life and death, and he remembers who he was before his marriage. He remembers himself as someone beyond all bonds and relationships. He sees how sometimes he coveted his wife when she was alive and now all the more that she is dead.

The man looks at the ground around him and feels a sense of responsibility for what happened to the beavers' homes, because of the tribe's interference, in the same way he understands his chronic sadness has been a burden for the tribe. At sunrise on the last day of his meditation the man gives thanks for the gift of his marriage and by doing so releases his sadness and the spirit of his dead wife.

When the man returns healed, the shaman gives him a drum and beaver pelts announcing his new name (Friend of the Beaver). Now the man will be responsible for finding the new water hole.

"You look happy. What happened?" members of the tribe ask him. The shaman calls for a tribal gathering at night fire.

"I saw that all of life is connected," he says at the fire. "We have to be considerate of each other and of everything in nature. While I sat next to the beaver dam I saw the truth. We disrespected the beavers' home at our last watering hole. We acted as though we owned the river, just as I thought I owned my wife's spirit. I will lead us to find a new watering hole."

In this manner the shaman has healed relationships on the personal, tribal, and ecological levels all at once.

While hundreds of books have been written trying to explain the role of the shaman, at the end of the day the shaman is still an elusive character, an outsider, and always a shape shifter. To some extent each one of us is a shaman, and everybody has talent analogous to shamanic ability. We all know a shaman or two. Witchcraft and dark magic is more common than it is mystical. We all know a witch doctor or two, and we can all act like *brujos* from time to time. And the spirit world, or being spiritual, is not separate from the physical world. Everything material is also spiritual. Perhaps the most important thing to remember is that our largest community issues on this planet stem from an absence of what we can safely call greater visions of harmony. The highest duty of the loving religion, the healing shaman, the priest, the pastor, the rabbi, the elder, the artist, or the scientist is always to create heaven on earth.

CHAPTER 8

ON THE BANKS OF LAKE WOBEGON

Growing up in northern Minnesota, I remember cold, gray sunsets across white snowbanks outside my living room window. Nighttimes my family listened to Garrison Keillor's deep voice on *A Prairie Home Companion*. I curled up underneath a blanket and cuddled with our family cat, TC. Our tabby cat was named after the logo on the Minnesota Twins baseball cap I wore around the clock when I was eight years old. TC stood for the twin cities of St. Paul and Minneapolis.

While Garrison Keillor cracked midwestern Minnesota jokes about small towns and Protestant Scandinavian churches, my mother made hot cocoa for me and my sister. We laughed at the stories from Keillor's Lake Wobegon while my father shoveled drifting snow out of the driveway.

My little sister was just a toddler. Sometimes, if it wasn't too cold, the two of us played together outside, making snowballs under the porch light while my father, in his big boots, lumbered heaps of snow back and forth. He would kiss my sister with his frosty mustache, and she would giggle or sometimes get fussy and swat at him with her mittens.

"Stop it, Dad. You're all wet," she would say. And she cried.

"You're a sissy," I told my sister. I threw snowballs at my dad's head, trying to take his attention away from her.

"Knock that off. Don't be a jerk."

The imaginary town of Lake Wobegon was thought to be near St. Cloud, just a short drive up the barren highway from the small town of Cambridge. My family had moved from Lydia in southern Minnesota to Cambridge in north-central Minnesota. Life in Cambridge was different from life on the prairie in southern Minnesota. The Rum River flowed across the edge of the little town of Cambridge, and the edges were marked by forests, lakes, and farms. Cambridge was cozy because of the dark woods and heavy snow on frozen tree branches in the winter. The little town was quilted safely away from the world, comparatively protected from the openmouthed winds and long prairies that rolled out from Lydia United Methodist into the Great Plains and Dakota Badlands.

There was a small viciousness that I remember about the northern Minnesota countryside. Coyotes screaming like babies during our walks in the woods. Owls snagging field mice. The word "frostbite." Even though the natural world was scary, the rules felt sturdier than the delirium woven into the very carpets, candles, and altars of the church sanctuary. The wilderness was continually my favorite place to know the world.

"If we want to see God, we need only look into our snowy back-yard," my father said from the pulpit. "He is naturally revealed to us in every river, tree, and snowflake. All we have to do is quiet our hearts and listen."

In private my father occasionally spoke of animal spirits, omens, and signs such as black crows on fence posts along empty wheat fields or deep fox prints in the black garden soil of the morning. Like the Native Americans who lived on the land in northern Minnesota before we did, my father believed everything was alive and full of wisdom. When we moved to Cambridge he built a tepee with his friend Gary, a Blackfoot Native American who owned property outside town. Gary wore his long black hair in a ponytail and smoked Marlboro Red cigarettes and drove a pickup truck everywhere he went.

"Son, do you see these prints on the snow?" My father guided me through a snowbank to see tiny paw prints tracking around the edge of the tepee poles. "These are mice that were trying to get into the tepee for warmth. This means that our tepee is a sacred place."

"Can we let them into the tepee to sleep?" I asked.

"If they come back, we'll let them in," my father said. "But they might be too scared of us."

"Why are they scared of us?"

"Humans are big creatures," my dad answered. "And we haven't always been nice."

Our tepee was filled with animal bones hanging from the poles, lashed with twine, feathers my dad found, and leather satchels filled with mysterious rocks and trinkets he collected while walking in the woods. Inevitably the items, myths, and omens he spoke around the fire surfaced in his sermons, cleverly disguised in the garb of current events, Christian theology, New Testament scripture, or local town anecdotes.

Overall, Cambridge was where I did most of my growing up, from seven to fourteen. Like the sarcastic epilogue to Garrison Keillor's "News from Lake Wobegon" always went: *Where all the women are strong, all the men are good-looking, and all the children are above average*, the human tendency to overestimate our own value and to underestimate our weaknesses was exactly what made Cambridge a safe place for me to explore the world and test its boundaries. As a preacher's kid I was both constantly admired and always suspected. In the Midwest this kind of paradox is a folkway sometimes called "Minnesota Nice."

When we moved to Cambridge from Lydia I was still a little kid, and I believed that everything in Cambridge was good to the core, like the salt of the earth. I didn't think about anything twice. I still remember some of the first moments these crystalline images of community perfection began to fracture.

"Dad, can we have popcorn?"

"I'll go to the concession stand at halftime. This is a big game, son. The other team is the Blue Jacket's biggest rival!"

My father took me to the high school football games every Friday night. The games were not only the largest regular community event in Cambridge but also one of the many gatherings my father was expected to attend. Usually a handful of kids from the church played ball on the varsity team, and it would be bad form if my dad wasn't there to support the Blue Jacket squad.

"Please, Dad. I want popcorn." I tugged on the sleeve of his poncho while he talked to the local churchgoers in the bleachers around us. I was eight years old. Rain fell from the sky. The field was muddy. The stadium lights shone brightly in the night, and teenage boys and girls walked around the stadium, some smoking cigarettes in the dark woods, some French kissing under the bleachers, the junior varsity boys watching the game closely in a group, adorned with their future varsity jerseys. The high school band played fight songs. The cheerleaders cried out, "We've got spirit, yes we do!" and the Blue Jacket players darted this way and that, streaking up and down the field and sliding tackles into the end zone for touchdowns, the entire town of Cambridge standing to its feet to cheer.

When my father returned with a tub of popcorn he was soaked. As he made his way through the crowded bleachers an angry man with a red face called to him from the aisle.

"Hey, Pastor. I'm talking to you. Didn't ya hear me? What are ya, deaf?"

I recognized the man from church, but his tone was different. I had never seen anybody angry with my father before (at least nobody except my mother).

"Put a cork in it, Rich." A woman from our church named Marge stood up and yelled at the angry man, pointing a gloved finger at him. The angry man held his hands out as if to say, "What, is the big pastor afraid?" and then he smiled a smile that said, "I win. He's a wimp." Then the man walked away, triumphantly.

A man from our church defended my father. "What does he expect if he abuses his wife? That she's not going to say something to her minister and church family? He's crazy! You only did your job, Pastor."

My father sat down in his seat, trying to remain professional. "Here. Take it," my father said. He placed the popcorn in my lap with an angry look, as if to say, "You see what you did. This was *your* fault." Then his face crumbled into sadness, and he patted me on the head as if to say, "Not your fault. I'm sorry."

Later that night when my father and I arrived home we stripped off our wet clothing in the entryway to the parsonage. My mother was sitting in a chair reading, and my sister was asleep already, still too young to go out on Friday nights.

"What happened?" My mother could tell my father was upset from the look on his face.

"Rich was acting like an asshole," my dad said. "He tried to confront me at the game."

"Oh, boy," my mother replied.

At some point I remember hearing adults at church say, "Rich can leave if he wants to. It's no big loss. He'll run 'cross town and join the Baptist church anyhow."

Our town football team was not the only squad deadlocked in bitter rivalry. It was clear to me that certain churches in town thought differently of each other. The lessons of this nature were never taught to me directly, however, and they were never explained outright. The differences between denominations were intuited or stumbled across, things overheard from personal counseling sessions, interventions, divorces, funerals, and marital affair headlines. I might be knocking on my father's study, asking him to come and play cards with me and my mom and my sister.

"I need time to myself," he would say from behind his closed door.

But instead of walking away, I would lie on the carpet and overhear telephone calls from church members, as if listening to a shortwave radio. Looking at the crack of light underneath the door, I heard bits and pieces. Words like "liberal" and "conservative" and "fundamentalist." I heard him say, "I warned them to consider it carefully before getting married," or "The woman's right to choose for herself is important." "We can do a private funeral ceremony, if you would like that. Sure, that's fine by me."

"Stop that right now," my mom would say. She would catch me lying near the door and pull me away. "Your father's work conversations are not for your ears."

"I want to know what he's doing."

"Church work is private. It's confidential."

Not understanding the hidden world of my father wasn't so bad at first. In my earliest memories my mother was great fun. A nighttime intensive care unit nurse, she took me to the video rental store on Friday nights, her night off, and checked out Disney films and classic stories. We watched *The Parent Trap* and *The Shaggy Dog*, *The Love Bug* and *Mary Poppins*, *The Sound of Music* and *20,000 Leagues Under the Sea*. She made nacho chips and cheese and bought decaffeinated soda. We stayed up late once my sister was asleep and watched our movies together. TC sat and purred on the arm of the couch.

On the weekends my mother took me to more eclectic events. Long car rides to the "cities." Shopping in Minneapolis and St. Paul, visiting art museums, and attending free community theater performances, even the occasional feminist lecturer.

One evening she took me to a Take Back the Night rally in downtown Minneapolis. I remember walking the cold streets and listening to people chant things I didn't quite understand.

"What are they saying, Mom?"

"They are saying men shouldn't hit their wives."

I remember the face of two white men in black suits standing outside a strip club that we passed. The lights blinking on the outline of a nude female body above the entrance. People holding signs and chanting at the club. The two men pointed at us and made machine gun noises, pretending their arms were automatic weapons. The people chanted louder. The bouncers laughed harder and cupped their hands over their mouths and yelled things back at the crowd.

"It's good for you to learn all about this," my mom said to me, and she held me tightly by the hand. "The world is a complicated place. And women are equal to men."

If I wasn't learning about feminism at an early age, then my mother offered me what she came to call "deals": If I read x number of books in y number of days, she bought me a video game. If I tried being a vegetarian with her for a month, she let me have friends over for pizza on Friday night, when the deal was finished. Always finding a way to teach me something and bargain against my lower boyhood urges.

As I grew older, my father was too busy to explain many important things to me; our visits to the family tepee dwindled, and he rarely woke me during the night to walk in the woods. At work more than sixty or seventy hours a week and always on call, he was too tired to play games or watch movies or come along for road trips to the big cities. Instead, locked inside his private study with its candles and jasmine incense, he played his acoustic guitar and read books until he was summoned on an urgent hospital visit or for a conference with somebody who needed to talk to him about something important. Every interruption of his privacy and quiet time outside work and parenting provoked him to anger.

Rebellion set in quite easily while I watched from the sideline as my father extended his help and guidance to the community.

I remember walking to his church office after school one afternoon during junior high school, eager to see him.

"Thank you so much, pastor." A young boy from the football team walked out of my dad's office door carrying a Washburn acoustic guitar in a black case. It was one of the guitars from my father's private study at home. One that I was not allowed to touch, and had never been invited to play.

"You're welcome. Make sure you practice like I showed you. Those chord progressions are the foundation of everything."

"I want a guitar, too," I said. "I want to learn how to play."

"Well. His parents are getting a divorce. So I am trying to help him."

"But will you teach me, too?"

"You never play your saxophone, and we bought you that. You need to prove yourself, first. You've got to show that you will practice."

I had wanted to play the saxophone only because Bill Clinton had looked so cool playing saxophone at his inauguration. I had imagined President Clinton playing it all the time, a kind of charismatic maestro of the United States, but my interest in the instrument quickly faded with the less than charismatic instruction of my middle school band director. For a long time before my dad let me play guitar, he invited young girls and boys from the church to give the most enthusiastic lessons and talks about the history of rock 'n' roll. I would interfere by yelling over the strumming.

"That's old people music," I would say. "Teach them alternative music. Like Nirvana!"

"Go to your bedroom," my dad replied. He held his guitar on his lap and pointed at me with one finger.

In light of the fact that my dad was not around, my mother was more annoying to me. When her career changed from nursing to teaching health and sex education at the high school, she tried regularly to talk to me about sex, abstinence, masturbation, pornography, and so forth. Her surgeonlike intellectual approach to adolescent male sex education, coupled with a feminist agenda and a slightly neurotic resurgence of conservative Catholic theology, which always surfaced when my father and she fought, caused us to bicker when we once had gotten along beautifully.

One night I forgot to finish the dishes. My father came home angry, which instantly escalated my mother's frustration with me.

"You're just plain lazy," she said to me, furiously scrubbing the dishes.

"Sorry. I forgot," I said.

"If you were sorry, you wouldn't have," my mother said.

"That doesn't make any sense," I said. "You're saying that people have to be perfect?"

"You gotta have the last word, don't you? Always gotta have the last word."

I wouldn't answer. Instead I pointed my finger at her with a smug grin on my face, as if to say, "You're the last-word freak."

"You're grounded," she said. "For the weekend."

When a father's practical teachings are absent, the frustrated son of a preacher sits in his pew and hangs on every single word spoken from the pulpit and every scriptural teaching his father shares with the congregation, projecting rebellious fantasies of biblical proportion onto the people in the pews, onto the minister, and father God.

Paired words like "father" and "son," "sin" and "savior," "crucifixion" and "resurrection" take on new meanings. Common biblical phrases like "There is no other way to the father but by me" or "Visiting the iniquity of the fathers on the children" were haunting. While listening to my father preach, I would leaf to the end of the Gospel stories and contemplate Jesus hanging on the cross, tortured, crying out, "Father why have you forsaken me?" and then in his final moment of acceptance, saying, "It is finished."

CHAPTER 9

HEALING CHRISTIAN WOUNDS

When I fell to my knees in the shower stall at the back of the lodge and left my body again, the last vision of my first ceremony began. Somewhere in the background I remember Ethan saying, "Ask Jesus to help you, Adam." I heard Cucaracha crying outside the mesa. Ethan started whistling a small *icaro*.

"*Limpia limpia, cuerpecito. Cristo cristo. Limpia limpia, cuerpecito,*" he sang.

In the distance, I saw a man in tattered rags and garments walking on the water. Although he was not familiar-looking, I knew the person was Jesus.

"That's Jesus," I said out loud. I pointed at him. It felt as though someone else should have been there to witness him along with me, an audience of some kind.

"Holy shit, that's Jesus," I said again. I looked around to tell somebody. Nobody was there. He was not pretty, sentimental, or fragile. Instead he was dark skinned and physically fit, like a carpenter. Although my words bore the mark of colloquial amazement, my voice was more honest than ever before. "Holy shit," I said again.

Then, still on top of the water, Jesus walked toward me. I never believed this was possible. In my most repressed thoughts, even during my most evangelical and born-again moments, I had always thought I'd have to see it to actually believe it.

The water in my vision rose higher. Jesus was defying gravity. The universe felt infinitely larger than me. I realized that boundaries and physical laws are not what they seem. They are not *always* true. Things are *absolutely* relative.

I fell onto my knees in the water, awestruck. I said, "Thank you." Although Jesus walked toward me, I did not look at his face.

"Thank you, thank you, thank you," I said. Over and over again, looking away from him.

Finally I saw his feet on top of the water in front of me. I knew he was expecting me to look at his face, but nothing had changed. Instead I was more afraid. For my entire life I had been so curious to meet this man and see for myself what he was all about. With Jesus standing in front of me, I was petrified. He was a person, not an idea, religion, or belief. He was a man with dry feet and cracked hands. He was not a theology, and he was not a doctrine or dogma. He was an enlightened being, some kind of highly evolved human being I had never been capable of imagining.

I said "Thank you" until the words blended together into a fearful moaning and golden oil poured out of my mouth and onto the surface of the water. Climbing into the air, the golden oil built itself off the top of the water into the image of a golden calf, shimmering before me, standing on the water between Jesus and me. I could not stop saying "Thank you."

Then Jesus reached down and lifted me onto the surface of the water. He placed his palm over my mouth gently, and I stopped saying thank you. He looked me in the eyes. Heavens roared and gateways opened in my heart. For the moment, I was no longer afraid of anything, and I knew myself fully. Bilocally, the music refrain, like a symphony of healing: *"Limpia limpia, cuerpecito. Cristo cristo."*

Then Jesus bent over and touched the golden calf. It dissolved. He looked into my eyes once again. I saw infinity in his pupils. Endless, seamless, loving, and true. Then I saw myself. Until I cried. There was lifetime upon lifetime folded into the only moment that I had ever known. I saw myself existing by the very act of choosing to exist. Realizing the unquestionable and ever-giving heartbeat at the core of reality. Beating over and over again. Pouring heart love from his eyes into mine. In one look his face spoke beyond words, and said, "Love me as your self. Do not make me into an idol."

When I returned to the mesa I cried on the floor of the shower. I managed to vomit one last time into a plastic bucket outside the stall and then crawled into a hammock, peaceful and easy.

Sunlight broke on the horizon. The rest of the mesa slept, snoring peacefully. Ethan crawled into a hammock next to mine. I felt my body, strong and alive, more alive than ever before. The last remnants of visions faded within minutes, and although my ceremony was over, I could never describe myself as "back to normal."

"One time I talked to God," Ethan said quietly. "It was one of the earlier ceremonies in my apprenticeship. And he told me: *Things between you and your brothers and sisters may not always be fair. But things between me and you will always be fair.*"

"I saw Jesus," I said. "I had no idea."

"Of course not," Ethan said. "How could you know until you found out?" He was quiet for a moment and then said, "I remember when Jesus talked to me for the first time. He said to me, *My father is the only one who has the right to judge anything, ever. And he never does.*"

"Thank you so much for your guidance and willingness to lead these ceremonies," I said.

"Two more ceremonies to go," Ethan replied with a grin. "More medicine. More cleaning. Next ceremony in twelve hours!"

I walked to the Amazon River by myself as the sun rose. I looked to the open sky. It was vast and blue with big white clouds. I held my hands in front of my face. The sun shone brightly and without any purpose whatsoever. Standing on the banks, I saw myself with new eyes. Then I dove into the muddy brown river water and baptized myself anew.

◻——————◻

CHAPTER 10

THE VOICE OF ONE IN THE DESERT

In at least a dozen of my ceremonies I've had similarly powerful interactions with Jesus. Because I grew up in the Christian world my visions of Jesus were especially healing. Although I am not a professional theologian or Christian historian, what I understand now about the person of Jesus will never change because of the visions I've had. When I first met Jesus in an ayahuasca vision, he was not who I was expecting. More than just the guru of a historical religion, Jesus was a multidimensional and highly evolved healer, more like a burning star or an enlightened being than the leader of an institutional religion.

In light of the fact that many of us live in what is called a primarily Christian nation, and in light of the fact that many people, like me, grew up in the Christian church, puzzled by the person of Jesus, it's important to consider a few questions. Would Jesus want people calling themselves Christians? And what does it mean to be a

Christian, anyway? My personal answers to these questions come from the heart of ayahuasca visions.

In subsequent encounters with Jesus I saw the man from the desert. I saw black starry skies and rivulets of sand moving across barren rock. I heard the echo of coyote cries on the mirage plains. I saw orange fires in the night and empty wells without water. In the plenum of emptiness I saw a dried-up desert womb, trying without success to create new life.

Where the face of God had been painted the serpent colors of ritual sacrifice, taboo, superstition, and fear, the Hebrew and Jewish prophets had intermittently predicted the coming of one who could crush the head of the venomous snake and restore balance. Having these ayahuasca visions of Middle Eastern ecology amid the symphony of jungle life, everything saturated, swimming, and overflowing with water, it was not hard to see (although he was first baptized with water) that Jesus' healing ministry was a walk through the fire.

Is it any wonder that his miracles were written about with such fervor? Raising the dead. Walking on water. Giving sight back to the blind with a single command. Who was I to try to understand the consciousness of such a man through scriptures and clumsy doctrines? As the famous world-religions scholar Allan Watts once said, "We should ceremoniously and respectfully burn bibles once a year."

When I saw Jesus I released my old Christian identity structure for something new. In one single moment, I was, as the apostle Paul wrote, "crucified with Christ." And the truth of love, not Jesus' love, not my love, not God's love for his special human beings, but love itself, was born in my heart. To proselytize the Christian agenda after my visions of Jesus, now, would be like looking back at the burning desert city of Gomorrah to become a pillar of salt slouching into thousands of pieces and scattered abroad by the dry wind of the desert. Because evangelism is not about someone promoting some "thing." Evangelism is a vibration in space and time that flows outward from a living communion with God, a God who is peace, harmony, compassion, and redemption.

Most often in my visions I saw Jesus in the wilderness, facing his demons. I would see him sitting on a mountaintop praying, having been baptized by John and crossing the Jordan River into the same wilderness the Hebrews had finally exited after forty years of wandering from Egypt. I would see Jesus praying for his forty days, maybe without food and water, without sleep, a self-chosen vision quest. I would feel the tenacity of this man's challenge to the people he met, of this man's challenge to me. The fierce eyes that gazed into my soul, saying, *Face yourself, and remove your sandals.*

The first temptation in the jungle mesa was my fear of death. *I cannot live without bread, without linear reality, without my body. Where am I? Oh God, I've lost my mind.* With a calm countenance on the jagged cliff, Christ remained steadfast in his prayer: "Man does not live on bread alone but every word that pours from the mouth of God."

The second temptation in the mesa would be to make demands. *Why does pain exist? Why should it exist? So much suffering. It isn't fair. Send me angels and make this drug trip stop. I will not believe anything until you first make it all go away.* Jesus said, "It is also written, do not put the Lord God to the test."

With my resistance weakening and my stomach turning over, my hands holding the rim of a bucket in the forest, the final temptation was to turn back and run, to take what I had seen and keep it for myself. *All right, I get what this is all about. I'm on top of this now. I'll tell everyone back home about the truth, and I'll never have to do this again. I've learned all there is to learn from this.* But Jesus, inside my heart, said, "Be gone. I am worshipping God." I lunged forward and screamed, screamed and pulled my hair, and then vomited into my bucket. By morning, as I saw visions of Jesus being attended to by angels on the cliff at the end of his forty-day vision quest, before his real work had even *begun*, I simultaneously watched translucent ivory linens falling from the heavens to coddle me and dress my wounds in the Amazon.

Over the course of drinking in ceremonies over the past four years, I've met people who have talked about Jesus the shaman and Jesus the visionary. Jesus the healer and Jesus the master. Whoever he was definitely, people who have seen Jesus in ceremonies mostly speak about growing to be like Jesus themselves, as opposed to focusing on what he "did" or "was" in some ultimate sense.

Accordingly, my relationship to Jesus' spirit is now personal, not religious. Based in moments of real physical crises and the most extreme mental resolve: to stay present and accepting of that within me which is dying, being at one with the vine of eternal life and letting the gardener prune my branches. Awakened by morning sunrise to the sprouting of my soul, squeezing up through the concrete of my fears, to live lightly on the surface of my body again, glowing like a smile.

Each time I sit in the humid tropical airport, waiting to fly above the palm trees and sail across the equator back to my American life,

I wonder: Will I be capable of living a holy life? Something I am proud of? How much *medicine* will I need before I am healed? How deep does my suffering go and how often must I return to the same struggles within myself? Should it be so hard to be happy in my own skin? When will I practice what I preach? And if I ask too many rhetorical questions, I can remember the instructions of Jesus, too, his rhetorical, teacherly response, "Consider the birds of the sky or the lilies of the field. They do not worry. And their father takes care of them."

CHAPTER 11

THE WALKING WOMAN

I remember sitting in Anderson's Drug Store on the corner of Main Street, seeing her pass in the rain with the hood of her jacket up over her face, scrunched-up nose, eyebrows dipping down like angry claws trying to gouge her eyes out. She was always talking to herself, sometimes looking like she was barking at herself or trying to bite off her own ear, like a wild dog. And there I was. I sat on one of the brown stools behind the counter, wrapping my hands around the icy tin cup filled with chocolate malt, watching the man in the white apron scoop ice cream, following the pink wheels of slushy turn inside the tank, always catching just the moment when she would walk quickly past the window.

I always saw her when I was out making trouble. I saw her walking through candy aisles while stuffing my pockets, in alleyways behind the movie theater while I smoked cigarettes with my friends, in the arts and craft section of Pamida while we used scissors to cut price tags off stolen clothing. Her fingers were always tangled in bundles of brown, white, and yellow yarn. She was always mumbling to herself. But I never really knew her.

People in Cambridge called her the walking woman. That was all she ever did. She carried a scissors and yarn in her pocket and clicked the blades back and forth in strange rhythms, always playing with her yarn, always cutting it into pieces. And though she spoke to herself quietly, with occasional outbursts, she never stopped walking. Maybe she was homeless. Maybe she was crazy. It always seemed to me like she was the only objective witness to the town of Cambridge. Like she saw everything for what it was. A private all-knowing eye.

"She is most likely a schizophrenic," my swim coach said to me. We sat parked in front of the Mobile gas station on the way home from practice. The walking woman passed into the gas station with the hood of her jacket pulled up over her face, her hands in her pockets clicking the scissor blades back and forth.

I sat by myself in the front seat watching her while my coach entered the gas station and paid for the gasoline. I hoped to witness some interaction between my coach and the walking woman, but nothing happened. While I waited I glanced beneath the driver's seat and saw an empty plastic wrapper with colorful letters. I picked it up and examined it.

"Playmate of the Month."

"Centerfold."

"Sex Secrets."

I quickly placed the plastic wrapper under the seat again. I had never seen pornography before. Strangely, my very first reaction was not sexual curiosity. I didn't immediately wonder about where my coach hid the sex magazine or its contents. Instead, I was excited. I knew a secret about an authority figure in my life who was also a member of my father's church. For the first time in my life it felt as though I knew something gritty about an adult. As if I had gotten past the closed door of my father's study and found a way to hear the names of the people on the other end of his telephone calls, seeing past the decorum of the Sunday school parade, the predictable smiles and firm handshakes, and into the surprising world I had always intuited the presence of but had never seen with my own eyes.

"She just walked around in there looking at things. I mean, really aimless," my coach said as he got back into the van.

"What does schizophrenic mean?" I asked.

"It means she has multiple personalities and voices living in her head. It's a mental disease."

When, only several days later, my coach accidentally fell into the pool while tracking us as we swam up and down the lane lines in practice, I was the first to defend his honor.

A school of boys treading water laughed at him. They watched him drag his wet body out of the pool in disgust.

"What a retard," someone said.

"That's a stupid thing to call someone," I said. "Mentally handicapped people have a mental disease. You have no idea how hard it is for them."

I preferred swimming to football because I was afraid of getting hurt. Secretly, in the football locker rooms, naked in the shower, sometimes I thought to myself, *I wonder if I look like someone who sucked dick when he was little? I wonder if I look like a girl?* Although swimming was a team sport, too, for the most part, the only person who could beat me at a swim meet was myself. While my father was a relatively absent life coach, save Sunday sermons, my swim coach gave me a form of advice every day. With the guidance of my swim coach, listening to him every single day, I broke two junior varsity records in the freestyle. If swimming wasn't only a seasonal event I might have stayed out of trouble.

"I've got the best idea," one of my friends said.

That was always how trouble got started.

I can still hear the decrescendo crashing of the football stadium lights shutting down one by one on Friday evenings after the Blue Jackets games. Autumn wood fires in the air and colorful leaves on the ground, not yet browned. I can see myself riding through the dark with the hood of my sweatshirt pulled up over my face. I can picture seven or eight of us boys on our bicycles gliding through the streets, our backpacks filled with soda and junk food and fireworks, looking for trouble. We lit a stink bomb on somebody's doorstep and rang the doorbell. We ran through backyards and over gated driveways. We hurled cartons of eggs at our English teacher's window and then shit on his car windshield. We shot bottle rockets at cars from the rooftops.

Whatever we did, it was about escaping at the last moment. It was about sprinting through the darkness, through gardens and alleyways, angry shouts trailing after us. "I'm calling the police on you boys!" It was about being heard but not seen, which was an obvious result of the fact that most of us boys were constantly seen but seldom heard.

Many in my group were doctors' children, bankers' and lawyers' children, teachers' and coaches' children; in a small town like Cambridge, we were the children of the public adults. Our pranks and acts of rebellion were mirror images of the dichotomy between our parents' careers and their home lives. It was about being suspected but never detected. When the lights went back up we were star athletes in our respective sports or honors students.

The only trouble was that we were not the only boys in the town of Cambridge. There were older guys, and there were boys whose parents weren't public figures. Some boys' fathers were drunks and thieves, dealers and burnouts living in the trailer park or the low-income apartments. These dangerous boys packed things like TNT, pistols, and rat poisoning into their backpacks. These rebels were both seen and heard. These boys said things like "Say it again, and I'll kill you." These boys were both suspected and detected. These boys were the first to get laid, the first to drop out of school, and the first to punch you in the face if you acted tougher than you really were. These boys didn't know about neglect or inauthentic behavior or hurtful feelings. These boys knew about raw anger and violence. Strangely, there was an admirable consistency to their behavior and tough outlook that almost felt sincere.

By the time I was fourteen I was frustrated enough to mingle with the real town troublemakers. My father sat my family down to tell us that we were moving to the big city of Minneapolis. He was taking another promotion to one of the largest Methodist churches in the state. His popularity was rising exponentially.

"This is a great opportunity," my dad said one night at the dinner table. "You'll make new friends, and we'll have a bigger house and more money. This is a blessing. You can both finish the school year in Cambridge. We won't move until the summer."

Within a few months I had stolen a pile of cash from the band office with a misfit named Mandy. She lived with her single mother in the trailer park. We got caught distributing stolen cash to our friends on the school bus. In the principal's office, Mandy admitted stealing the money. I tried to blame everything on Mandy, acting like the good preacher's kid, and earned myself a suspension from school and a visit to speak to a probation officer named Mr. Wade.

I sat in his office during the fall. It was windy outside, the way it gets right before it's going to snow.

"Why did you steal the money?"

"Well, everybody makes mistakes," I said, trying to sound reverent like my father. "I've asked God to forgive me, and I won't do it again. I've learned my lesson."

"I don't believe you. I think you believe you can get away with anything because you're used to getting away with everything."

I was lucky that Mr. Wade was a member of my dad's church. I heard my father talk to him on the telephone asking him to give me a break that same night after I visited the juvenile detention center.

"Go easy on him," my dad said. "I'm at the church all of the time. We just told him we're moving. The news has been hard for him. He'll come around."

I returned to school unscathed and doubled my efforts. I began to steal from church members' houses when my family visited for dinners. I used the bathroom and stuffed my pants full of cologne and exotic lotion. I rummaged through drawers and took spare cash. I bragged to my new friends, who were more trouble than ever, "My dad got me out of it last time. Nothing is going to happen. I'm the preacher's kid."

I took my father's keys to the church at nighttime and snuck into the sanctuary. I smoked stolen cigarettes and drank stolen beer. I used his keys to unlock the soda machine. I filled a pillowcase full of quarters, and I took spare cash from the offering plates in the church office. Whatever I was not getting at home I took for myself at the church.

"I've got an idea," I said. It was the first night the two groups of boys would mingle: the popular misfits and the real troublemakers. "Let's break into my dad's church," I said. "I can show you guys around, and we can take soda from the machine."

We rode our bicycles to the church after the Friday night game. We talked about which girl we had French-kissed under the bleachers. It was never the girl we thought we would kiss. It was just somebody. Somebody different outside the world of notebooks and bells on the hour. Suddenly you had body urges and you pressed your face against hers. "You kissed Kelly! That's weird, man. Why would you kiss her? Was she any good?" And one of the boys from the bad-boy crowd said, "You pussies need to get laid. French kissing is for babies."

I opened the sanctuary doors with my father's key and led the boys inside. Reaching the altar together in the dark church was like an actual religious moment. Everybody got really quiet and afraid we were doing something sacrilegious.

"You guys don't have to be scared," I said. "It's not as holy as it looks."

"I don't know, man. I don't feel like we should be doing this," one of the boys said. He was fidgeting with his hands in his jacket pockets. I lit a cigarette and sat on the steps of the altar.

"I do this all the time by myself," I said. "It's no big deal. If there is a God, then he's not doing anything about it." I cupped my hands over my mouth and tilted my head to the vaulted ceiling. I yelled, "God God God. If you're there, then make a noise!"

"C'mon, man," somebody said. "Cut it out. Let's go egg Mr. Schmitty's house. I don't want to get into any trouble."

And just like that the two groups of boys were united by a common cause: getting the hell out of the church. After all, rebelling against authorities was one thing, but rebelling against the church, against God, against the town's institutional moral power house, that was downright scary to every single boy in Cambridge. And so, united under one banner, all the boys left the church to go make mischief together. Everyone but me and this other kid. One of the bad boys had stayed behind with me. A kid named Jeff.

We smoked Camels and didn't talk much. I showed him around the church with a cigarette hanging from my lip. "This is the choir room where the singers hang their robes. And this is the fellowship hall where everybody eats after church."

It was quiet and boring, almost methodical. We didn't stay long after I gave him the tour. We didn't know each other too well. He didn't seem that tough when it was just the two of us. I probably didn't seem that spoiled or snobby, either. He seemed sad, and I probably seemed lonely.

"Should we go find the rest of them?"

"They're down at the Rum River," I said. "They've got dynamite."

As we mounted our bicycles to find our friends and make trouble again, I noticed somebody walking in the autumn moonlight. There she was with her hood up over her face. The walking woman. She was talking to herself, and I could hear the clicking sounds of the scissors in her pocket. Something about the way she never changed and always kept walking scared me. Standing next to the church, stolen money in my backpack, I felt like the walking woman could see straight through me.

"I'm going home," I said.

"You sure?"

"For sure," I said. "It's too cold anyway."

Although it was still months before I would leave the little town of Cambridge and move to the big city with my family to yet another parsonage and yet another new church congregation, I remember how that moment felt more like good-bye than all of the rest.

CHAPTER 12

SINS OF THE FATHERS

"Did you mark the coordinates?" My grandfather's radioman sat behind a tall boulder and bit into an apple. As he ate, he imagined rucksacks and empty railcars while he looked into the gray clouds lingering high above the mountains at the border between North and South Korea.

The two men, a forward observer and his radio operator, had crawled miles from their platoon to the site of a peasant village said to be housing weaponry and secret North Korean militia. Having called back the village coordinates to the U.S. mortar bombers, the two men waited to confirm the village burn.

"You want a boy or a girl?"

"Firstborn was a daughter," my grandfather said. "Next one better be a boy."

"What will you do if it's another daughter?"

"I suppose I'll have to teach her how to split wood and work the land. Someone *by my very name* is gonna learn hard work before I die. I can tell you that. I'll name it after me, even if it's a girl."

The two men laughed together. My grandfather drank water from a green canteen. Then screaming whistle sounds crossed the sky above their heads. The two men looked through their binoculars at the village.

They saw burning green pine trees and people zigzagging in the confusion. Barefoot runners flying between screaming and flashing white-out booms. Chickens flapping upward into the empty air. Shrapnel daggers chasing the helpless people. And fire.

"Boy, I hope them weapons are in there for all this trouble," my grandfather said.

"Screw it," his operator said. "I don't care. I'm just following orders. Let someone else think about it." He put down his binoculars. "I can't take watching it anymore."

My grandfather continued to watch. As he scanned the attack, his binoculars found their way to the outskirts of the village. The last straw hut built of mud and thatch, on the very edge of the village, caught fire. Sitting in the yard of the hut was an old woman in a rocking chair. Although her home was burning, she rocked back and forth, back and forth. Her leathered skin was wrinkled and worn cold from many decades beneath the jagged peaks. She looked to my grandfather like she was steeped in some kind of magic. Perhaps the forgiveness of warm rains and brooks from the deep rivers in the springtime, the green bulbs and white tulips rising from the dark soil, just after the heavens finally settle and the ground opens.

She rocked in her chair while the village burned around her. She refused to react. To my grandfather she looked misplaced. As the roof of her home crackled and burned, it suddenly fell on top of her. She caught fire. Her angel-white hair was pure flame. But she did not move or react. She just sat there. She died in her rocking chair just the same, rocking back and forth.

My grandfather couldn't stop looking at her. At first he thought, *I shouldn't be here. This isn't right. I didn't sign up for this.*

But his radio operator said, "Hey. Take a load off. Pull a few drinks off this whiskey and catch some *z's.*"

As my grandfather rested in the shadows of the giant boulder his last thoughts before drinking himself to sleep were, *Jesus, I can't wait to have a son.*

Of course I don't know what the radio operator said exactly or what the sky looked like. I don't know exactly how it all happened because I wasn't there. But each time my grandfather tells me that story, he mentions how he couldn't stop watching her. He doesn't say, "I couldn't stop watching her in the rocking chair." He says, "She was burning alive, and she wasn't doing anything. Just sitting there." Then he's quiet. He looks off into the distance of his mind and says it again, "She just sat there." Then after more silence he shakes it off and says, "They were supposed to have hidden weapons and militia in that village. Boy, I was excited to get home. I knew I would have a son. I kept telling myself that."

I always ask my grandfather, "And what happened to your radio operator, again?"

"He wouldn't keep quiet. He was always complaining and jabbing. He ended up getting shot in the face one day by the Koreans. I told him to hush up, but he wouldn't listen. He was too cocky for his own good."

Inevitably, I've painted a picture in my head that helps me empathize with the heaviness my father faced when he came into this world. A shell-shocked and alcoholic father. A twisted sense of paternal duty. A heavy feeling of guilt mixed with violence. However, the hopeful part of my grandfather's war story hasn't been forgotten, because whenever my grandfather tells me his Korean War stories he always ends with his last story from the war, the last one before he came home and created my dad. I'm not sure if he knows that he always ends his Korea stories with my favorite one, but it never fails.

For several months before my grandfather left Korea, after returning from the front lines in the mountains, he adopted a small boy named Kim-Yang from one of the war-dead villages. He took care of the Korean boy and kept him on the military base. He tried, naively, to bring the boy home with him to the United States, but there was a conflict between him and some of his men and commanding officers. My grandfather masks his affection for Kim-Yang's memory and tries to end the story by saying "He was just our little platoon mascot. We let him stick around." But in the end he always adds, "I wonder what ever happened to that little guy."

CHAPTER 13

LA DIETA

In order to train in the ayahuasca healing arts, shamanic apprentices raise their consciousness. It is not enough to learn a songbook and have visions of God to lead an ayahuasca healing ceremony. During the course of an apprenticeship, a shaman cleans his body to the core and also masters his mind in order to harmonize with every thought, action, word, and emotion that could come up during a ceremony and potentially interfere with his duty as a doctor.

An ayahuasca apprentice will learn to direct each ceremony by means of a heightened sense of intuition learned over time and the guidance of medicinal plant energies. Apprentices bond with plant energies through plant diets and ayahuasca ceremonies combined. The healing plant energies are expressed and channeled by vocal articulation. The medicinal plant energy is literally encoded into the apprentice's body and expressed through medicine songs or *icaros*. Shamans are taught *icaros* by the plants themselves.

By way of entrainment or psychic attunement to the shaman's *icaros*, purges and healing visions manifest in the patient's body and mind. At the beginning, an apprentice's first goal is to sit through ceremonies from start to finish with a straight spine and balanced breathing, matching his voice to the songs of his teacher's. Inevitably his first challenge will be his resistance to the medicine flowing through him. All resistances, all fear, will be burned off by the refining fire of the medicine channeling through the container of his body and his mind. He may spend many ceremonies purging on the ground, but when an apprentice finally learns to stay present and can quietly observe the medicine working through his mimesis (singing along with his maestro's *icaros*), the medicine will yield specific practitioner techniques to be used co-creatively with the medicine's current. When shamans do things like bilocate or shape-shift into different forms (such as a hornet or a jaguar) during a ceremony or when a shaman receives his own medicinal healing techniques and personal *icaros*, it is because the ayahuasca medicine imparted the gifts as it cleaned and passed through the channel of the apprentice's body. Ayahuasca shamans will eventually bilocate or shape-shift into different spiritual forms because they are capable of being both directive and receptive at the same time, addressing a number of different psychic dimensions, energy currents, and patients throughout the course of one ceremony.

Most fundamental to the ayahuasca practitioner training is a revolving participation in medicinal plant diets. Spending long amounts of time in isolation among the healing trees, ingesting healing plants, ayahuasca apprentices will purify at faster speeds. If plants grow toward the light, taking in sun, and making themselves out of it as they go, then ayahuasca training by healing plant diets follows the same growth pattern as more and more light enters the body and mind.

Master ayahuasca shamans complete dozens of these rigorous plant *dietas* and drink in hundreds and hundreds of ceremonies before graduating to a mesa of their own. I remember first desiring to become an ayahuasca shaman, and I remember my first plant *dieta*.

When I arrived at El Puma Negro for the second time the camp had moved upriver and was only an hour outside the city of Iquitos, Peru. Whereas my first group had included six people and a daylong river trip, two buses and porters took thirty-five of us to the new camp. The lodge had expanded, multiple bungalows had been built from the ground up, a meditation and craft center had been erected, and jungle hiking trails had been blazed conservatively for walking.

After a major magazine article featured the miraculous healing ayahuasca tradition at El Puma Negro lodge, flocks of people traveled to Peru to drink ayahuasca. At camp for my second trip, enrolled in the training *dieta*, I met Ethan's teacher, Domingo, for the first time. He was looking over my diet.

"Maestro!" Ethan bellowed, emphasizing the "o" sound like a salutatory bugle blast as he ushered our group off the bus. A short Peruvian man walked slowly up the path to meet us, holding his hand up in a casual greeting. Ethan shared a warm hug with his teacher and then turned to us. Since Ethan's eldest teacher, Arturo, had passed away only weeks before, I expected Domingo and Ethan to be in a somber mood. Instead, there was nothing but strong smiles and good spirits.

"Wait until you see Domingo in action," Ethan said to me. Then he said to the group, "Adam thought he had a healing adventure when he was here last year, and Domingo was out of town. You only had half the fun!"

"Oh, wonderful," I said, sarcastically. "This will make ego death so much less frightening!"

"Adam did some good work last time," Ethan said. "And he'll do some good work again this time."

Mentally preparing myself to drink ayahuasca all over again, I reflected upon leaving Iquitos after my first round of three healing ceremonies, standing at a large fountain in the city square at night, telling Ethan I would be back to continue my healing work, and giving him the largest thank-you of my entire life.

Ethan had replied, "Just wait until you work with Domingo next time you visit. Wait until you see my teacher in the medicine. People call him the nicest badass on the block."

Looking at Domingo standing in large rubber tapper boots with a baseball cap and a taciturn Peruvian smile on his face, I couldn't help but remember the phrase and repeated it a few times in my head, contemplating the necessity of my upcoming *dieta*, "The nicest badass on the block."

While we sat in a circle at the first plant diet ceremony, a day before our first ayahuasca ceremony, the birds settled into the quiet and the crickets stirred on the edge of the forest. Shadows hung like black curtains in-between green foliage. Soon the jungle would be entirely black. The only sounds would be those of animals stomping in the distance or the buoyant bouncing of a bird call, back and forth, back and forth, like drips of water from a faucet.

Each *dieta* ceremony was thirty minutes long. Not everybody at camp dieted. Some were only drinking ayahuasca. Those of us who were dieting took turns drinking our plants after Domingo had blessed them for us.

"What is your name?" Domingo asked me in broken English.

"Adam," I said. I felt sheltered and typically American for knowing only one language.

"Adam," he repeated. He looked deeply into my eyes. Then he began whistling an *icaro* into my glass of plant juice. This lasted several minutes.

"*Salud,*" he said.

"*Salud,*" I said before tilting back the cup. I took four big gulps and then cringed and wiped my lips clean. "Tastes like pepper," I said.

"That's sanango medicine you taste," Ethan said from a nearby hammock.

The brew of *dieta* plants contained every plant in the ayahuasca brew except for the vine and leaf (the two elements that open vision for ceremonial work). However, it is not accurate to say that drinking *dieta* plants without the vine and leaf in the brew was a "normal" experience. Within thirty minutes of drinking my peppery-tasting glass of cloudy-white plant juice, it felt as though somebody had siphoned the life force out of my body. I was extremely tired but stuck in a wakened stupor, like being sick but not capable of falling asleep. Everything felt extremely sensitive, from the sounds of people talking, to the creaking of feet on the mesa floorboards. I felt feverish, but my body temperature was not elevated.

"The plants will make their home in your body," Ethan said, as if on cue. "They will clear out crossed energy and do a lot of straightening. At first it can feel toxic, but that's because they're making changes. They'll talk to you about it if you ask them."

"They actually talk?" I asked.

"They chatter," Ethan said with a sly grin on his face. He swung in a hammock near the back of the mesa as Domingo guided each person through the ritual of drinking his first *dieta* cup.

After the *dieta* ceremony was over, I wandered back to my bungalow. It was still early in the evening, but a heavy sleep fell upon me. While lying on my mattress, behind mosquito netting, I thought to myself, *It's too early to be this tired.*

"Oh boy, it's a mess in here." A voice came from inside my head, somewhat animate, as if an exaggerated elf or dwarf from a fantasy story were talking to me on a secret miniature radio hidden in my ear.

"You did a lot of drugs, didn't you?"

"Are you kidding?" I said out loud.

Then I heard a host of chattering followed by a beautiful song, the sound of a lullaby *icaro*, and then Ethan's voice coming from somewhere, saying, "The *icaros* come from the plants. They teach the medicine songs to apprentices through the diets. The *icaros* come from the plant teachers themselves." Then it was morning, and the sun was rising. Parrots screeched back and forth, and hints of mist sat on the perimeter of the jungle. The walk to breakfast felt like a mile. My body was heavy, and I felt angry and irritable. Before I could wonder about the plant voices that had talked me to sleep, I heard them again.

"Objectification of women. Drug abuse. Lying. Arrogance. Religious piety. Family history. We're making notes, son!" I couldn't help but laugh out loud as I walked the dirt path to the longhouse for breakfast; it was strange to be in an altered state of consciousness outside an ayahuasca ceremony, and I almost expected that visions would appear and that I would need to keep a purge bucket by my side.

Right when I arrived at the longhouse, the morning gong rang loud and spread through the camp like ripples on a pond. Ethan and Domingo sat with their apprentices around a table, already eating.

"*Buenos días,*" Domingo said.

"*Buenos días,*" I replied, clumsily. I was the first person awake in the camp, but how had I known it was time for breakfast only minutes before the morning bell sounded? Usually I was a heavy sleeper.

"Boy, you were right, those plants like to chatter. It's strange to hear voices sober," I said. I felt awkward using the word "sober," afraid I was being offensive. Then I added, "Well, not entirely sober. It's hard to describe."

I'm not sure what I had hoped for, but the table of shamans and apprentices smiled as if to say "What did you expect from a shamanic plant diet?"

By noon I was sleeping again and there were no signs of energy in my body. I felt as though I wanted to vomit but had nothing to puke up but my soul, which was too big for my mouth. After the second *dieta* ceremony that same night and five more hours of afternoon sleep, the first ayahuasca ceremony of the week commenced.

"I feel like I'm burning alive," I shrieked.

Sweat poured down my body from head to toe. I found myself stranded in the middle of a desert, the mesa hovering somewhere above my head, far, far away. I spoke out loud, interrupting the *icaros* for a solid hour, trying to verbally manage my experience and intellectually outwit an astronomically sized visionary whirlpool.

"I am afraid of men touching me. I'm scared of what people think about me. Everybody is always watching me. Are any of you my friends?"

I threw my hands up in the air and shook my body back and forth and grabbed my face and screamed at the top of my lungs. There was no meaning. There were no visions. There was no symbolic interaction of visionary "things" and meaningful teachings, moments to sit and reflect or time to purge. The act of purging was the simple and profuse expulsion of verbal diarrhea and terror.

Things like "God doesn't love me. Hell. I'm in hell. I can't make decisions. I don't believe I exist. I am not good enough to exist. I feel schizophrenic. Stop the madness," and then screaming again and then tremors and getting down onto my knees and begging the earth below me. "Please, somebody, help. Please. Make the voices go away!"

At one point, I said, "Oh, Jesus. I feel like I'm going to die right now. This is the end!"

Ethan came to my side and said, "Then you have to fight, Adam. You have to fight."

Upon hearing Ethan's voice I calmed for a moment and realized I had overstated the severity of my situation. I said with a moan, "I AM SUCH A BIG LIAR. I AM THE BIGGEST LIAR OF ALL TIME."

"Yes," Ethan said. "But mostly you exaggerate." The entire mesa roared with laughter.

As if my body reacted exactly to the truth of his statement, I began to sweat out lies and exaggeration. The sweat was hot and I felt like I was dying, but most important, I felt simultaneously cool inside. A paradox. The heat of my physical body was both severe and not that bad at all. A physiological feeling of exaggeration and lies at the same time. Then I blurted out again.

"I feel like I'm burning alive! No, wait, it's not true. I'm fine," I said.

"We'll let you cook a while, and see what happens," Ethan chuckled.

Immediately a child spoke out of me, and I saw myself as a very young boy, scared of spiders, heights, and other boys.

"Yeah, okay," I whispered. "I get it."

From that point on, although my sweating continued, it ceased to bother me. Several minutes later, Ethan and Domingo laughed and spoke back and forth to each other in Spanish, and then Ethan called one of his attendants.

"Juan!" he called. "*Agua en la cabeza de mi hermano Adam.*"

"*Sí,*" Juan replied. Then a short Peruvian man named Juan poured cups of water from a large bucket over the crown of my head.

"Over your bucket," he said in broken English. "Your head. Put your head over bucket." Then Juan put his hands on my head and gently rinsed my scalp. For the next hour of the ceremony, as Juan continued to rinse my head with water, I had the most remarkable vision.

Juan's hands disappeared. I stood close to a waterfall somewhere in a green valley. Sitting naked on a rock in the sunlight, I examined my body closely, looking with curious eyes like I had never truly seen the details of my own flesh and blood.

Looking at my hands, I saw each small pore and the boundary between each neighboring pore. Each knuckle, each cuticle, each wrinkle, a distinct part with distinct boundaries. Flowing together seamlessly, the same animate life dwelled in the fibers of each compartmentalized section of my hand, like a small animal that was somehow a part of me, respondent to my wishes, and then also separate, capable of being taken away, capable of doing things in its own mind, capable of doing things that might be *involuntary*.

Then I saw my legs, my toes, my knees, the hair on my arms, and my entire body. The details illuminated. I saw realms of my body exhibiting the highest intelligence and individuality. They had voices. I saw the totality of my body, down to cells, and veins, and blood, and water, and organs, and joints, and wrinkles. It was something called "me," and it was comprised of billions upon billions of individual conscious entities.

"Everything is made of spirits," Ethan said back in the mesa. "All structures are spirit and contain spirits, and the structures themselves are also spirits. We are constantly calling them in and out of our bodies and minds. When we think, or act, or feel. When we eat or have relationships. At our jobs. We are always interacting with spirits. We are made of spirits."

Then I saw my faces. Many different faces within my face. I saw the spirit of unhealthy sexual craving, the face of a glutton. I saw the spirit of addiction to non-nourishing food. I saw the spirit of dehydration. I saw the spirit of dependency and jealousy in dating relationships. I saw the spirit of frustration. One by one, I saw the spiritual characters in the cast of my life as energies held in my body, my joints, my skin, my hair, my lips—the living presence of all the different images of myself and the sounds of a waterfall rushing through each one of them. As the visions of my different spirits appeared one by one, they began to coalesce. When a large enough mass of the toxic characters congealed, I found myself lunging forward to vomit or dry heave or say "Help." And Juan would continue to pour water over my head.

"How you feeling, Adam?" Ethan asked me several hours later.

"Clean," I said.

"That's the spirit," Ethan replied. He squeezed my shoulder affectionately as he left the mesa, whistling while he sauntered back to his bungalow to sleep.

When the kerosene lantern was lit after the ceremony, many in the circle sat in the mesa talking and whispering to each other. The crickets chirped softly in the jungle. I reflected upon the ceremony with a smile on my face. Later when I drifted off to sleep in my bungalow, I heard the same little worker voices, saying, "Out with the bad, in with the good. Out with the bad, in with the good. We're cleaning it up real nice in here. You got a television set in this place?" I laughed.

"Sorry, sorry," the voices said. Then one of them said, "We don't generally watch television. That was a joke." Then I burst out laughing again.

"Okay. *Shhh. Shhh*," they said. Their voices trailed off and mixed with strange and beautiful *icaros*, like the plant spirits were vanishing into a jungle somewhere in my body to do more work and to wake me in the morning.

CHAPTER 14

PRAY WITHOUT CEASING

In the New Testament epistles, the slightly neurotic but always char-ismatic apostle Paul wrote to the people of Thessalonica, urging them to "Pray without ceasing." In the Gospel of Matthew, Jesus similarly instructed, "Do not let your left hand know what your right hand is doing," and also, "When you pray, do not pray like the hypo-crites, for they love to pray standing in the synagogues and on the street corners to be seen by men. . . . But when you pray, pray in the secret."

One of the primary stressors of the Western world is mental dark-ness. When we hide our true feelings behind niceties, mannerisms, or sarcasm, we create mental darkness. When we speak one thing but feel a different way, we create mental chaos. When we live one way but feel guilty or unsure about it inside, we create tension in our lives. When we attempt to create self-worth by our thoughts, beliefs, or possessions, we feel anguish. Chaos, tension, and anguish are each exemplary degrees of an absence of light in our consciousness.

But darkness is never as powerful as the light. If our consciousness were ever pure darkness we would not be able to perceive darkness. Therefore, we cannot ever have an experience completely absent from light. In order to see any form of darkness whatsoever, no matter how pitch black the darkness gets, we must have the tiniest degree of consciousness, the tiniest degree of light, to perceive darkness in the first place. In other words, there is no such thing as nonbeing, unconsciousness, pure black, pure evil, or nothingness. Goodness and light illuminate the darkness all of the time.

An ayahuasca ceremony brings more light than I've ever seen or even imagined possible to my darkest places and secrets. The illuminating effect of ayahuasca medicine on the psyche catalyzes healing. If Jesus and Paul were here today and could bring light to anything specific, I believe they would illuminate the false idols we have placed upon the altars of our lives.

When Paul said to pray without ceasing he addressed a new group of Christian converts in Thessalonica. The people of Thessalonica wanted to know how to follow the teachings of Jesus, which Paul had shared with the people of Thessalonica during his travels. When Paul mentioned the practice of Christian prayer in his epistle, and instructed the people of Thessalonica to pray without ceasing, he was preaching about doing something without legalistic obsession or self-righteousness.

Similarly, when Jesus instructed people to pray in the secret and not let the left hand know what the right hand was doing, he was encouraging people to be themselves without premeditation, without "trying" to be something in particular, without "trying" to appear holy. To both Jesus and Paul, holiness was life itself. The Gospel of Jesus encourages us to stop trying to make life anything more or less than exactly what it is in this moment. When there is only one moment, our prayer will be the experience of living in the now. The experience of living life in the now is the same thing as life eternal: a place where we are at one with our father and heaven is already here.

Paul's message to the Thessalonians and Jesus' teachings about prayer are still relevant. In Western cultures, false religions heavily outnumber the healthy ones. Anything we think will cause happiness we pursue madly. Once we have the happiness, the happiness dies, and we look for another way to create happiness all over again. The American dream of a house and a family and money. The dream of fame and wealth. The right car. The hipster art and music collection. The right graduate degree. The right travel abroad program. The above average marriage. The best sex. The right diet. The beautiful body. The most consistent yoga practice, or the most devoted meditation. Even the most holy religious life. But the truth is that no matter how hard we try, we cannot escape the fact that we are already saved, already perfect, with nothing to prove.

Therefore being a Christian, Hindu, Muslim, or Buddhist means occasionally letting go of our religious idols for the sake of life itself. Nobody has to stop going to church to release false idols. Nobody needs to quit his job tomorrow or sell every material possession he owns and dance naked in the streets. The only thing required of us is that we live openly and honestly with one another, already knowing that everybody is already everything they need. Forgiving each other constantly and remembering we don't have to sit to meditate, we don't have to kneel to pray. Our honesty and authenticity, without our premeditation or effort, is the answer every single person is waiting to hear since the moment they meet us. It's the universal evangelism, the answer to every question, the work of creating heaven on earth.

And sitting down to be silent and reflective, say, just once a day, doesn't hurt.

CHAPTER 15

PLAYING INDIAN

The suburbs of Minneapolis were like night versus day compared to the rural towns of northern and southwestern Minnesota. I toured our new house when it was still bare. The parsonage was three stories with hardwood floors. A big garage outside and a rolling green hill in the backyard that sloped into a forest and swampy pond. Directly behind the pond was a freeway. I could see the steeple of the Methodist church from our back porch or from the rooftop where I would sit at night writing in my journal. Instead of bird calls I heard the sounds of cars on the freeway. The nicest cars crept through our cul-de-sac and subdivision: businessmen driving Mercedes, BMWs, and Audis, and teenage boys with aviator sunglasses driving Mustangs and convertibles, the bass beat of expensive stereos vibrating through the neighborhood.

Right away my father put the family tepee in the backyard and hosted the first church Fall Festival. There were carnival games in the church parking lot, and if you walked to our backyard from the church you could sit in the tepee and drink hot apple cider and have your face painted. The tepee was open to anybody.

"You're really putting it in the backyard?" I asked. My family sat at the dinner table irregularly even during our first months at the new suburban home. Everybody felt out of place.

"It will be a good way for people to get to know me," my dad said. He seemed like the only one excited about the suburbs. "Plus there isn't any land around here for me to keep the tepee. Would you rather not have it at all?"

As I grew up, my father's interest in Native American ritual and the outdoors had become less about intimacy and more about show-and-tell. Our tepee was the special field trip for the district schools in Cambridge, and more often than not my father hosted small adult gatherings in the tepee without me or my sister.

What was once sacred and private felt like a cheap play toy, a plastic relic used to show off my dad's eclectic spiritual interests. My favorite legends were shown off at the pulpit and for my classmates, the spiritual messages less cloaked because of fewer conservative church members and my dad's increasingly popular image. When my family finally moved to the suburbs of the big city, the cultlike shadow of our family tepee and its guiding presence in my psyche all but disappeared.

"We need to get you signed up for football and swimming again," my dad said one evening, arriving out of breath and late to the dinner table.

The night before football tryouts I asked my parents which one of them could take me to the field. My mom taught high school full-time and was working part-time on a counseling internship in Minneapolis and finishing her master's degree in psychology at a private college in St. Paul. My father was at the church nearly seventy-five hours a week. We hardly saw each other.

"Walk to the field with your cleats," my dad said. "You'll be fine."

When I arrived at the field in the morning and saw a hundred boys twice my size, dressed in gear twice as nice as mine, I turned around and walked home. Frustrated, I played my guitar in my basement bedroom. Although my father had finally taught me how to play the guitar, he rarely had time for lessons in the suburbs and often got irritated by my slow progress. He would impatiently improvise loud riffs and intricate finger-picking patterns over the noise of my clumsy strumming.

A week after tryouts, my dad finally said something while sitting in front of the television at night. "How were football tryouts?"

"I didn't go," I said.

"Decided not to play, huh?"

"I wouldn't have been starting anyway."

"You don't know that. You never know what could have happened. Were you afraid?" I didn't answer.

"Sports won't matter to you ten years from now. I still have my books and music but not a thing to show from being an athlete," he said. "My dad wouldn't even let me play senior year. He made me quit football and basketball to help him work the land. Be thankful I don't make you work like he did. At least you can do whatever you want."

"I think you should still go out for the swim team," my mother chimed in. She was highlighting passages in a psychology textbook, eating walnuts and drinking red wine. She looked at me over the top rims of her reading glasses.

In the suburbs, drinking alcohol had become normal for my parents for the first time and occurred on a regular basis, especially when they got home from work at night. Occasionally they would fall asleep on the couch in their clothing. When my mother got particularly buzzed she would laugh to herself and recite cheers from her Catholic high school cheerleading squad.

"We've got spirit," she would say. Then she would stand up and spread her arms into different geometric patterns in the air. "Yes, we do!"

The day I quit the swim team, after only several months of practice in the suburbs, I was home alone making dinner for myself and my sister. My mother called while I was supposed to be at practice.

"Why aren't you at the pool?"

"I quit," I said.

"I'm too tired for this. You're old enough to make your own decisions. Have you made supper for your sister?"

It was in the small moments that my family first grew apart. It would have been easier if there had been events to mark the change, something any of us could point at or talk about. Like the evening my dad came home early from a staff parish board meeting and caught me exploring his private study, touching and examining all of his trinkets and playing with his electric guitars.

"I don't want you listening to my music, and I don't want you playing my guitars or taking my books. I'm putting a lock on my door. You have a job. Buy your own things."

"But it's not like I'm going to break anything. I don't have enough money to buy anything like this. I work at a bookstore for five bucks an hour!"

The harder my dad worked at the church and the more stress he put on himself, the more elaborate his private studies became. Each house we lived in contained a private study that was an evolution of his last. The eccentricity of my father's musical instruments, compact disc collection, and book library correlated perfectly with his workload at the church and his personal depression. In the suburbs, where the church work was more businesslike and less relational, my father's study was more eclectic than ever.

I still remember the inventory of his suburban study in the same way that certain smells evoke strong emotions. It smelled like sage, incense, patchouli oil, and cigar smoke. It felt safe and warm. He had an old leather recliner chair and a Pioneer stereo. Bands like Pink Floyd, Buffalo Springfield, The Byrds, and The Band sat on the wooden shelves, propped up by masonry bricks. There was a statue of the Buddha and a Navajo painted cow skull on the wall. Books with titles like, *Thus Spake Zarathustra*, *The Dharma Bums*, and *The Collected Poems of William Blake* rested earmarked on his bookshelves and coffee table. Each item in the study felt important. It was a place he went after work when he was tired and didn't want to talk to me or my sister or mother.

"But he doesn't share anything," I complained to my mother.

"You wouldn't like it if we came into your bedroom all the time and took your things."

"I don't have anything cool. Besides, you guys already have a bedroom. Why does he get two bedrooms?"

"He doesn't let me into the study, either. And he doesn't care if you promise to return what you borrow from his room. He says no to me, and I'm his wife. So give it a rest. Okay, honey?"

We all knew that his study was so much more than a little room he had decorated. It was the place he went to remind himself that he was not his family, and he was not his church, and he was not his job, and he was not his life, and he was not his duties or his kids. My entire family knew that's what the study and the books and the scotch and cigars were all about. The study was about my dad not liking the way his life felt on the outside.

One night at dinner I said, "It feels like you don't want us around. You go into your study and get all depressed, and—"

My father stood up and slammed his fist on the table. The silverware rattled.

"You too, huh? What do you people want from me?" He stormed out of the dining room into his study.

"Leave it alone," my mother said.

When my father grew his hair out and got his ear pierced and bought a Jeep Wrangler with oversized tires and a big stereo and began to say things like "I don't care what anybody thinks of me anymore," my mother drank more red wine and started sharing her disapproval of my father's behavior.

"Your father is having a midlife crisis. I don't spend a penny on anything but this family, and he's out buying toys, acting like it's the 1970s. He doesn't care how it's making me look. How it's making this family look."

Behind every unrecognized moment of hypocrisy was the perpetual disintegration of my family's nuclear bond, and the motor driving the fission was my father's emotional dissociation from his career as a Christian minister and his life as a suburban father and husband.

When Bill Clinton came on television for a special appearance and pointed his finger at America, saying, "Even presidents have private lives," I felt certain that something bad was going to happen. I knew the president was adulterous, just as it was clear to me by looking at my Dad's book collection that he was not interested in his life as a minister or father. He was interested in pagan gods. Although I had no hard evidence against him, I began suspecting he was having an affair.

"You have no idea how demanding these people are. It's not even a church any longer. It's a corporation. I'm a CEO dressed up like a pastor," I heard my dad complain to my mother behind closed doors.

"Well, we need to get the kids through school. It's not fair to keep moving them around."

"When I was a kid, *we moved*. You get used to it."

"Have we ever gotten used to it? Don't we always say how we wish we could relax or be back home in Michigan?"

"Whose side are you on anyway?"

And I couldn't blame my father for wanting out. The Valley Sheppard United Methodist church ran a private preschool and kindergarten program out of its basement and was in the middle of selling a piece of property it owned across the street in order to settle a million-dollar debt. Not to mention its apportionments to the Methodist conference were years overdue. My dad had become a business manager.

The choir director, a dramatic New York musical artist named

Susan Looney, resigned after kicking a chair over in rehearsal and throwing sheet music at her singers. Like his name indicated, the Native American youth pastor, Raymond Dunnadda, had no real youth programs for me to get involved in when my father first arrived (Raymond Dunnadda also resigned). And the associate pastor, Fred Burglebee, dressed up like a clown one Sunday morning by surprise and sang to his wife for her birthday in front of the entire church without asking my dad for permission. After a number of similarly nutty incidents, Mr. Burglebee finally resigned, too.

In the wake of these healthy housekeeping staff changes, my father's popularity oddly decreased. For as many colorful employees at the suburban church, there were just as many colorful parishioners with colorful opinions. The congregation was well educated, liberal, suburban, scatterbrained, and wealthy. It became regular in a church of nearly a thousand members for my father to lose people for things as silly as the topic of a sermon preached or the selection of music for a particular time of year, let alone the coming and going of ineffective staff members.

The values of the suburban church often reflected the suburban fragmentation: hasty rides in minivans to sports practice, cell phones and pagers ringing, lives on call, stressful vacations, too many hours at jobs not loved, and marital affairs.

In order to escape the parsonage, I attended conservative Jesus camps during the summertime. At first my dad was skeptical of my desire to go to the camps. Having been recruited by evangelical Baptist kids at school, my father worried I would be influenced by rigid thinking. Perhaps his redeeming quality, despite his being at the church most of the time, was his ability to let me think and make decisions for myself.

"Are you sure you want to fill your head with all that fundamentalist, Bible-banging crap? Those camps are *ultra*conservative," he said. "I try to be open-minded. I let you think whatever you want, but I've also got to look out for you."

"Well, at least there aren't a million people, and I don't have to pretend like I care about all of your *clients*," I said.

"*Clients*," my dad mused. "Well, I suppose it will be good for you to make new friends."

The summer Jesus camps were kind of like religious therapy. I met other kids just like me. It was a place where all the teenagers whose parents belonged to one big church or another came together to get out of the suburban rat race. Strange things always had a way of happening at Jesus camp.

"I summoned you to this hilltop because the Lord has called your name!"

I was sixteen years old, and one of my camp counselors, an elderly churchwoman named Ruth, talked at me with her King James Bible. She wore white slacks and a black T-shirt that read "Abortion Is Murder." The sky was dark green. Droplets fell from the clouds. We stood on top of a grassy hill looking out over the belly of a stormy lake. A wooden cross and small altar for morning worship songs stood behind our backs.

"We must plead the blood of Jesus over this camp," she said. "There are going to be tornadoes if we don't plead the blood of the lamb over this bible camp right now."

During the week Ruth had convinced me I was different from the other campers. At one of the campfires, during a time for prayer requests, I mentioned my father was a pastor, but I didn't think he was a very *good* pastor. I shared my suspicion that he was having an affair and that I felt neglected at home. Three other preachers' kids echoed similar sentiments about their fathers' ministries. The next day Ruth singled me out and walked me to the lake. We sat on the edge of a sunny dock near the cold water, and she explained to me a vision that God gave to her.

"I saw it last night in my dreams, Adam. You're going to lead a revival," she said to me. "You will try to fight it for a long time, but eventually God will have his way with you and you'll become a pastor. You're going to be the pastor and preacher your father isn't ready to be yet. You will lead your dad back to God. Have you been baptized?"

"My dad baptized me when I was little."

"Did you accept the holy spirit?"

"What do you mean?"

"Did you speak in tongues?"

Ruth insisted that my father's baptism had not been authentic, and she insisted that my father was not a real Christian because neither he nor I spoke in tongues. She said it was his fault, not mine, that I hadn't been introduced to Jesus properly.

"I work in the Methodist church because I'm calling home the lost sheep from the fallen denominations. The Methodist church is a liberal and sinful place. They don't teach the members to speak in tongues and ask for the spirit when they convert."

She argued with me, using scripture after scripture, that a person can be redeemed only after he has received the gifts of the Holy Spirit, and he begins to speak in tongues. She said this meant that hardly anybody in the Methodist church was actually saved.

"It's the holy prayer language," Ruth explained. "True Christians know how to speak it, and you're going to begin speaking it by the end of this Bible camp. Before you leave this camp you will be a true disciple of Jesus Christ."

Standing on top of the hill in the wind and rain, she said to me, "Adam, it's time. Close your eyes. Lift your hands to the sky and let the Holy Spirit speak through you."

I remember feeling afraid, like I was going to disappoint Ruth, or worse, I would admit to Ruth I figured she was full of shit, that all the Holy Spirit talk was twaddle. But then something happened.

"Like this," she said. She lifted her hands and closed her eyes and shook and moaned. Then she expelled the most unusual language I ever heard.

"Ho-ta-mu-kay-alay-lan-tu-nay," she said. And whether or not it was the emotional palpability of her outcry or whether I was just sixteen and confused, I will never know. Whatever the noises meant, they resonated, like someone was daring me to let go, like throwing chairs into brick walls or dancing when nobody is looking. Something in her strange noises and hands lifted to the sky in the wind and rain, and the way she looked like she just didn't give a fuck about anything, made me want to join. As if taking myself by surprise and hurling myself off a tall mountain, I fell on my knees and lifted my hands to the heavens.

"Oh-rah-be-no-may," I yelled, over and over again. "Oh-rah-be-no-may." Then I lay on my back in the wet grass, looking up at the dark green sky. I cried so hard I momentarily forgot why I was crying. Even though I didn't know what I had said, if it was tongues, or if I was a real Christian, or if it was going to make Ruth happy, or if it would push the storm away, or if I was only pretending, or if it was that I missed Cambridge and hated the suburbs, or if I wanted to know more guitar chords, it was an emotional release.

"Thank you, Jesus," Ruth said. "Thank you, Jesus. This victory belongs to Jesus and nobody else. We bind the devil in the face of other religions on this planet. Fallen denominations like the Methodist church. And we call one more soul back to the true God." Ruth prayed angrily, as if she were casting a protective spell over me.

Before I returned home that summer, I stayed on to be a counselor for the younger kids at the Bible and drama camp. When I finally went back to the suburban parsonage, and after recovering from a nearly fatal venomous spider bite, fundamentalist Christianity made a lot of sense. Life after death was real, and my father seemed to be losing his faith. I sought order and structure in the first place I found outside my home. Fundamentalist Christianity sat me down and told me the black- and-white difference between good and bad. Told me how to end up in heaven after I die. It was exciting. It gave me a feeling of confidence and self-importance (not everybody learns to speak in tongues on the top of a stormy hill, or has a near-death experience, or the opportunity to evangelize to his father the preacher). Since there is no rivalry more charged than fathers and sons, the bitterness at home grew exponentially when I left my father's church and became a Baptist fundamentalist on the other side of town.

I carried my Bible with me wherever I went, condemning and

correcting people just as "lovingly" as I could, assured that people everywhere were going to end up in hell if they did not convert to not just the Christian Gospel but the Baptist Pentecostal doctrines I had subscribed to. Earmarked in my New International Bible was a passage where Jesus rebukes the Pharisees for their lack of faith in his healing abilities, saying, "A Kingdom divided against itself cannot stand." To me, my father's everyday absence in my life was indicative of the quality of his faith. He wasn't a "real" Christian anymore.

And I knew better than he did. I studied Baptist theology rigorously, determined to outsource my father's entire ministry if I could. We spoke with great academic indifference toward one another in the short passing moments we came together, like two theologians debating the truth of the universe calmly, with contempt for one another on the inside.

"So tell us why you stopped coming to our church?" my dad asked, a little sad. Two of my parent's friends sat with my family on the porch eating dinner with us. My mother poured wine into goblets around the picnic supper table. The suburban moon was pale white in the night sky. Cars droned in the distance.

"I like it better," I said. "I actually like going there. I might get baptized again at the Baptist church."

"Those churches are based on fear, son. We've talked about this, pal," my father said, becoming arrogant, as if we had a close and open relationship. He winked at our guests. He stood calmly at the grill turning shish kabob skewers over the fire, like he knew something I didn't.

I thought to myself: *You're a fraud.*

CHAPTER 16

THE WORD BECOMES FLESH

The jungle chimed like little handbells. It was the first time I had heard the new bird sounds in all of my visits to El Puma Negro lodge. I was drinking my second *dieta* and was in the middle of my third ayahuasca ceremony of the week (my ninth ceremony overall and my third trip to Peru). It was quiet in the mesa except for the birds and the sounds of Ethan and Domingo whistling playfully. The ayahuasca ceremony was nearly over. In the rafters of the mesa a pod of pink river dolphins swam playfully in the vision space.

"It's the *icaro* of the pink river dolphin," Ethan said. Domingo chuckled and puffed on his *mapacho* cigar.

"They're beautiful," I said.

When I closed my eyes I saw myself riding on top of one of the dolphins, soaring through outer space. And when I opened my eyes

I could see the mesa. The moonlight pooled in the lodge windows. The smell of tobacco hung in the air, and the sound of Ethan and Domingo's whistling, like a sonnet, propelled the pod of dolphins in the waters and the colors above my head.

"Adam," a voice said to me. The voice inside my head was not my own.

"Huh?"

"Will you tell Marcus that Richard is here and that I love him?"

I thought about it for a second and remembered a man named Marcus was in the mesa, too. I reflected on Marcus for a moment in the quiet. We had spent time talking throughout the week at camp.

"When I came back from Vietnam, I started inventing things," Marcus had said to me one day.

"What did you invent?"

"Different energy-saving devices. I was thinking up ways to go green."

"Did you ever sell a patent?"

"No. They weren't interested. Of course now I see similar things on the market, and I'm somewhat disappointed."

"At least you were ahead of your time."

"I don't know about that. I think a lot of people had the same ideas back then. The government can be slow to get behind the right thing."

"Slow," I said. "That's gracious of you."

"We come around," he replied. "I've learned to put trust into the process and see the good on this planet. Never hated the government, myself. Frustrated, sure. But I try to stay hopeful."

"Did you lose any friends in Vietnam?"

"I did," he said. And that was all. We rocked back and forth in hammocks, spending the lazy afternoon hours napping and chatting.

"Who are you?" I asked the voice in my head. When I closed my eyes I saw violet-colored wave bands emanating outward from the heads of the dolphins. The dolphin pod was gathered in a circle, and I saw myself sitting in the center, cross-legged in outer space.

"My name is Richard."

"And what do you want, exactly?"

"I'm a friend of Marcus."

"How do I know I can trust you?"

It was eerily quiet, and Ethan's *icaro* had stopped. "How do I know I can trust you?" I repeated the question.

"I'm a friend of Marcus. Please tell Marcus that Richard says hello. Please tell him I love him."

"Ethan," I said.

"What's up, buddy?"

"There is a spirit talking to me, I think."

"Well, tell it to go away if you don't want it around."

"I would, but he wants me to tell Marcus something," I said.

"Me?" Marcus said from across the mesa.

"What does he want you to say?" Ethan asked. His voice was calm and unaffected. Domingo cleared his throat.

"His name is Richard, and he wants Marcus to know that he loves him." It was quiet for a moment or two, as if the message was being uploaded somewhere.

"Thank you," Marcus said.

"Thank you," said the voice in my head. "Thank you for your help." Then it was gone.

After the ceremony I sat with Marcus next to a kerosene lantern, and we talked into the night. "So what was that all about?" I asked. I waited for Marcus to speak.

"I was going back into my childhood," Marcus said. "Thinking about old friends and this little town I moved away from when I was nine years old. My best friend Richard at Boy Scouts. I never saw him again after we moved. I wondered about him years ago when I was in Washington, D.C. I visited the Vietnam memorial wall, and I figured Richy was my age so maybe he enlisted. Turns out he did because I found his name on the wall. Died in combat. Boy, it tore me up inside. I hadn't seen Richard since childhood, like I said. During the ceremony I was thinking about that little boy I used to be, and that small town, and my old friends, and I was feeling a little bit alone inside. Then you shared that message you got. It was good timing. Very interesting."

"Do you think that was really his spirit?"

"Maybe. Or maybe it was like psychic intuition, and you felt that I was thinking about him and the medicine wanted me to feel comforted. Who knows?"

"Yeah, I guess it doesn't matter."

"The mind is a mysterious thing," Marcus added.

We sat next to the protective little flame of the lantern that night for quite some time, and we didn't say much to each other, but, then, we didn't need to. I wondered if I was submitting myself to ideas and experiences too strange. Although I was peaceful I felt unsure of my experience. *What do I make of all of this? How could I ever share any of this when I get home without sounding crazy?* I rubbed my fingers together, anxiously. Marcus must have noticed because his comment seemed to answer my thoughts.

"Doesn't matter what other people think of you," Marcus said. "It's important to trust yourself and whatever you make of things. Trust that what you come up with can help people. Trust that if it doesn't help people that it's not going to harm anybody, either. Don't take anything too personally, if you know what I mean."

Several tears rolled down my cheekbones. It was meaningful to hear a grown man like Marcus address my concerns, not coddling me but reassuring me with a gritty bit of wisdom and a kind but not overbearing smile. "Thank you," I said. "I trust you," I said. "That feels good to say. You know I've always heard therapy-type people and Christians talking about 'trust issues' in relationships. I didn't really know what it meant."

It was true. Until that night, I had always been told to trust in people or trust in God, as a command, as a duty, something I was inherently bad at and needed to learn to do properly. Feeling trust without trying or being told to do so and loving how good it felt changed something. The word "trust" became real to me: *the way you feel when you are trusting.*

The more I drank ayahuasca during that *dieta*, the more words lost their intellectual definition and gravitated toward what feelings the words actually signified. Words, as the writer of the Gospel of John put it, "became flesh."

CYNICISM AND RESENTMENT: THAT WHICH
ATTEMPTS TO BLOCK MOTION

"But what if it isn't this way?" a woman asked during the middle of the ceremony. "Excuse me," she said. "Excuse me. Stop that song and answer me."

Ethan and Domingo stopped shaking their *chakapas* and whistling. They said nothing.

"I see peace and harmony in these visions. We're all connected; I can see that. I'm having a million thoughts. I see a million things. But I'm not going to believe this is true because I remember a world filled with hatred and violence, and it's really fucking hard for people. I'm lucky enough to come down here to South America and do this. So my question is this: What if this isn't so?"

"If what isn't so?" Ethan asked.

"All of this," she said, desperately.

"Be specific," Ethan answered.

"This!" the woman raised her voice. Then she grabbed her hair and her cheeks and clutched at her hips and her chest. "This!" she cried again.

"Being resentful and cynical means thinking something shouldn't be the way it is, and that is a frustrating way to exist in this world," Ethan replied.

The woman began to plead. "Please help me," she said. "HELP!"

Domingo walked into the center of the mesa where the woman sat, suddenly having a panic attack. "This, this. ME!" she screamed. He shook his *chakapa* in the air above the woman's head.

"Domingo," she said. "Please help me."

"*Sí,*" he said. "*Todo está bien.*"

Then he cleared his throat. Like magic, a large crack of thunder split the sky above the mesa.

"Oh, thank you," the woman said as he began to sing. Then she said, "Thank you so much."

And although there was not one more clap of thunder that night, and although it did not rain one drop, a deluge of tears poured into the mesa. While Domingo sang, the woman found water springing up from a dry and barren place within her. A place of faith and belief running through her tears.

"I shouldn't be the way I am. I don't even like myself," she said. And then she cried harder, and harder, and harder, until she vomited several times and finally lay back down on her mattress with a sigh.

The next morning she didn't look like the same person.

She said, "I had no idea how much I resented everybody and everything and mostly myself. I hadn't cried in years. I was so *stuck*. You can't cry when you think everything and everybody is wrong all the time. It keeps you from thinking it's okay to cry. Resentment keeps you from accepting love, and cynicism is such a total joy sucker. But I had no idea. I knew the words I was speaking last night, but then I didn't. And then I didn't know myself. And then I did. I'm probably not making sense, but this is the best morning of my life."

"Domingo doesn't say much in ceremonies," I said. "But I guess he doesn't need to, huh?" Everybody laughed.

Although it was her experience, it was mine too, and all of ours. We all knew what she was talking about.

READINESS: A REFLECTION OF HONESTY

"I can't do this!" I screamed.

"Say that you're not ready," Ethan said. "Own your feelings. Instead of complaining, say that you're not ready. Complaining makes things worse. Honesty makes them better. So stand up and say you're not ready for this experience. Try being honest."

Summoning more courage than ever before in my entire life, I got to my feet despite the powerful effects of the ayahuasca.

"I."

"Am."

"Not."

"Ready," I said. Each word felt like a hammer pounding through a wall inside me.

"Now you're doing the work," Ethan replied. Domingo chuckled at me and began to sing a new *icaro* in Quechua.

"*Limpia limpia, medicina,*" he called out.

Finding control, I sat back down. I didn't know what was supposed to happen next, but the honesty I had summoned made me feel ready. Each time I wondered if I could make it through the night, I found myself releasing my fear by repeating the strongest words of readiness I had ever found within myself: "I am not ready."

"Readiness is a reflection of your ability to be honest," Ethan said. "That's all it is."

The teaching was not an intellectual idea or something I could read somewhere in a kung fu trainer's manual. It was not the *Karate Kid*, and it was not a book about Zen that somebody told me to check out. It was a real teaching happening in the midst of a terrifying experience. It was a real teaching I could understand firsthand for the rest of my life. And when I thought of how I could tell people back home of my experiences, I knew there was only one way. I would say, as simply and straightforwardly as I could, that "I am not ready to understand every ayahuasca experience I've had, and I may not know how to talk about what I've seen in my visions, but I will share what I've witnessed, and I'll share what I have understood about myself as honestly as I can."

Sensing my accomplishment, Ethan added, "I mean, look at it this way, Adam. From one perspective, you drink foul-tasting jungle juice and talk to Jesus while vomiting down in the jungle. I mean, how can you really be ready for something like that?"

CHAPTER 17

ENTRAINMENT

Ayahuasca is not a cure-all. A typical journey to drink ayahuasca in Peru may only include between three to six ceremonies over the course of several weeks. Because old temptations are bound to re-surface, and relapses can always still occur, daily spiritual practices are necessary for a lifetime of personal growth.

After returning from the jungle and trying my hardest to stay centered, several times relapsing into old familiar patterns yet re-turning to work with ayahuasca to strengthen my resolve, I received instructions necessary for leading a balanced life outside ceremo-nies. These are incredibly simple things I do every day in order to keep my mind and body entrained to the teachings I learned. My list was received from plant spirits and visions throughout the course of approximately fifty ceremonies and several plant *dietas* over four years (most of which took place in Peru).

1. The cornerstone of my daily practice is meditation or quiet time. It was the first thing I learned to do when I returned from Peru, and it led to the development of the rest of this list. "Meditation" is a word with far too many stereotypes, religious mystery, and sentimental values attached. What I mean is that once or twice a day I sit quietly by myself, and I close my eyes and focus on my breathing for thirty minutes. When thoughts or feelings or words or visuals come into my mind, I shift my attention back to the sound of my breathing. By doing this in private I learned to do it during stressful public situations, which has helped me to be less reactive and more reflective and empathetic in everyday situations. Being empathetic, I feel connected to life.

2. I drink a lot of water. One time in ceremony I saw that most of my body is water, and I saw the effects of dehydration. Lack of water puts my entire emotional, mental, and physical being into a state of vulnerability. I drink more water than anything else because it purifies me and keeps me focused and centered. When I feel stressed out, I drink a big cup of water and focus on my breathing.

3. I stretch out. I practice yoga regularly. But even more important than practicing traditional yoga— the ancient postures, the volumes of Vedic sutras, mantras, and Eastern philosophy—is the upkeep of my physical body. Yoga is a beautiful science that both focuses the mind and teaches the body to stay centered. It is a great complement to meditation. Regardless of the niche culture of yogis and gurus, stretching out the body and circulating blood and oxygen, being physically active, is important. It reinforces

the truth of evolution and optimism and progress, and it drains the accumulation of negative energies. That being said, I like yoga better than "working out" because when I work out I tend to think about my image so much. I enjoy yoga. It's a personal preference.

4. I sing. When I shower in the morning, when I am walking, or when I am traveling between major daily events, I will sing or whistle uplifting melodies. I focus on carrying confidence in my voice and staying in tune and pitch. By singing throughout my day I reinforce the idea of push and pull: that between major solitary events is a seamless flow connecting all events. Music connects everything for me. I like my guitar. I am also careful not to let music take control.

5. I write. Writing is my favorite meditation practice. This book has progressed through 1,000 pages, four drafts, and hundreds of hours. It feels simple and clean because a lot of disciplined work has gone into it. The final draft of 250 brand-new pages came out in roughly twenty days. Over four years and many ceremonies, I have learned to write each day for several hours. My writing has evolved beyond what I thought was possible. My writing has given me a voice to guide all of the lost, angry, bitter, or sad voices in my head. Writing has given me better visions of the past and future. My writing only improves.

6. I eat healthy. I eat three meals a day. In the morning I drink hot tea to warm up my digestive system, and I eat fresh fruit and oatmeal to give me good energy. Then I eat a large lunch, the largest meal of the day, when the

sun is highest in the sky. (This is how it's done in the jungle. It's not a theory; it's just practical to take in the most energy when you need it the most, at midday.) My meals are greens, natural protein (nonmeat), and grains. I avoid sugar, grease, caffeine, and heavy food. At dinner I eat a smaller version of the same. I don't multitask while eating. I eat only until I am almost full, and I chew my food mindfully. I often follow both meals with tea to help stoke the fire of my stomach so that I can quickly integrate the energy of my food. I recycle and try to shop as organically and "green" as possible.

7. I practice celibacy. I don't mean that I never have sex or that I think sex is bad. When I am in a relationship I simply make sure that my periods of sexual intimacy are balanced with times that do not rely upon sexual interaction. Too often my relationships have grown stagnant or stuck when they relied upon sex as the catalyzing act of intimacy. Orgasms drain a lot of energy and are part of a biological program that makes babies. That mating program becomes viral and causes infidelity and sexual addiction if it is not mastered. The mating instinct needs to balance with a bonding instinct. It's good to share physical intimacy without the goal of orgasm. It's not moral or prescriptive. It's just my way of keeping things balanced.

8. I read and write letters. I avoid television because I find it stressful. Instead I read a variety of news sources, and I read books. I enjoy reading and writing letters with as much care as I practice creative writing. It is a way to keep strong remote bonds with the people who shaped

me. In this way I stay in a spirit of gratitude for the web of my life.

9. I have fun. I like to share intimacy with like-minded people who are walking similar paths. From time to time it is important for me to laugh, to cuddle, to not take anything seriously, and to poke fun at myself and others. To kiss. To not have any plans. To sit next to fires or go hiking. To be in the wilderness and without any agenda. To give and receive compliments and to collaborate in random acts of creation. I also pay off debts quickly and live within my means.

10. I like to work. It is important for me to constantly connect every aspect of the work I do to loving thoughts and good intentions, whether I'm in a ceremony or not. If I mess up, it's important to forgive myself or ask for the forgiveness of others and then continue working. Working on myself flows naturally into everything else. I love good work.

CHAPTER 18

VIRGIN STAR OF THE SEA

In the small town of Cambridge, I had been a popular student athlete. But boys at the suburban high school called me a faggot in the hallways. Although I was without friends, I refused to hang out with other social rejects like me, even when I was invited. Instead I kept my nose and pencil in a notebook, avoiding eye contact with my peers, especially boys, and writing angry or contemplative and self-important poetry about the church, about God and the jocks at my school (though I secretly wished I wouldn't have quit playing sports).

I remember one afternoon with heartbreaking clarity. I played my guitar and sang at my school talent show and received a loud swell of cheers and screams after performing an original love song I had written. Walking down the hallway after the talent show, my cheeks bright red and my chest roaring inside as if I had discovered fire for the first time, I felt like things were looking up. A cute brunette girl named Julie talked to me during English class after the talent show.

"You're super talented. Why are you so quiet all of the time? All you do is write in your notebook."

"I don't know," I said. "Thanks."

She smiled at me.

After English class two boys cornered me in the bathroom.

"I saw your autobiography paper. You got a "D" for turning in poetry. You're not supposed to be in honors class. Just because you think you're special and write in your stupid notebook all the time doesn't mean that you're a genius. It just means that you're a pussy and a faggot."

Before I was given the chance to respond, the other boy shoved me backward. I fell onto the floor. My head hit the concrete. The two boys walked away, laughing.

"Fa—got," they called. "Fa—got."

A goose egg quickly swelled up on the back of my head.

When Julie started dating one of the boys several days later, I kicked a hole in my bedroom wall.

As my frustration accrued, the major theme of my creative endeavors was the quest for female love and companionship. All of my poetry was romantic. All my journaling addressed my future wife, "dear you," "sweet dream girl," "future wife," as if she were the sole audience and would be given each page on the day of our wedding. In classes all I could think about was having a girlfriend and lifelong partner, someone to see me, to know me, to love me. The idea of a soul mate became idyllic for me, a single point of focus expressed in meter and steel-string-guitar chords. The sentimental teenage blues.

"Why don't you write about Nature? Why do you always write songs about girls?" my mother asked.

"Why do you always have to ruin my life?" I replied.

My mother's attempts at curbing my romantic idealism and budding sexual impulses most generally made me want to punch something. No matter how wise or keen her approach, I could sniff her coming from a mile away. Unfortunately, my mom taught sex education to my confirmation class at my father's church, which I was forced to attend despite my crosstown love affair at the fundamentalist Baptist church.

My mom would come to class with diagrams, overhead projector slides with fully colored, anatomically correct pictures of the male and female reproductive systems, videos of childbirth, and always the notorious "question box."

When the "question box" was passed around to collect the scraps of paper on which the students in confirmation class had written their questions about sex, I waited in a cold sweat for someone to embarrass me. Instead of asking "Can you get an STD from masturbating?" someone might ask, "So you and pastor had sex to make Adam, right? Was it good-quality sex that produced Adam?" (One cannot explain the embarrassment of having a parent teach your entire class about private parts and *intercourse*.)

Being a high school anatomy and physiology teacher, a former nurse, and a pastor's wife, however, my mother knew how to say things about private parts and God in one sentence without making anybody mad. The dilemma was that my mother was a strong advocate of abstinence, which made it impossible for me to submit my question the year I lost my virginity.

When I lost it I was in my grandfather's house trailer with my girlfriend, Lauren. I was sixteen. She came along with us on our family vacation to visit my grandparents in Michigan. Whenever we wanted to suck face we snuck outside to the house trailer, which was parked in the yard because my grandparents had recently arrived home from a moose-hunting trip to Alaska.

It was the usual hot-and-heavy making out one afternoon until she asked me, "You want to do it?" Instead of answering I began breathing fast and somehow fumbled my way into penetration and ejaculation within a matter of three minutes. With my body pressed awkwardly on top of hers, she made painful noises at first.

"Ouch. God, that hurts. Wait. Stop."

"Are you okay?"

"Okay. Yeah. I'm fine. Keep going."

"Are you sure?"

"Don't talk anymore. Just go."

Then she made a moaning noise I had never heard firsthand, like the kind in pornography films. Just for a second, it seemed like I was a porn star myself. I was going to be incredibly good at sex, right out of the gate. Lauren was a popular girl who should not have been dating me. She dated guys on the baseball team. My sex skills would clearly make all the difference. All of a sudden my eyes got big, and I quickly pulled out to avoid ejaculating inside her. I fell off the trailer trundle bed with a loud thud, my jeans twisted in a mess around my knees. I convulsed and grunted as I came.

Lauren laughed at me, and there were little blood spots on the sheets between her legs.

"We just lost our virginity in a trailer," I said.

"You popped my cherry," she said.

"I popped your what?" I asked.

"You know, my cherry," she said. She pointed at the small flecks of blood on the sheets.

"Sorry, my mom didn't cover 'cherry popping' in her sex-ed class at church," I said.

We snuck off to have sex in the trailer every day for the rest of our vacation, and at the beginning I wasn't worried about anything. It was brand-new. We discovered our bodies together in backseats and movie theaters, breaking into my dad's church with his keys and making out in the quiet sanctuary where nobody could hear us. The only problem was that we weren't married, and soon I heard my mother's voice, like a psychic bird of prey, talking to me about "pre-marital sex" and "abortions," and "unwanted pregnancies," and "divorce rates." When Lauren's period was several weeks late, my question for the confirmation sex box would have been "Are abortions legal in Minnesota? Do you go to hell if you have an abortion? How can you have one without your mother finding out?"

The day Lauren went to the Planned Parenthood clinic I called her on the telephone. I had planned a big speech about telling our parents the truth and asking for help, but when I heard her voice on the other end of the phone, I forgot what I had planned to say.

Out of nowhere, I said, "Maybe we could just have it and get married. We love each other, right?" There was dead silence.

When I didn't hear her say anything I knew that it was over and that my first love was going to be a piece of my history. Just the way things happen like that, where you can feel yourself looking back at the moment years later, as a grown man or woman, right as it's happening, like you're standing outside time looking into a double-mirrored room.

"We don't even know if I'm pregnant. I'm probably just late," she said. She hung up the telephone. For the next four hours I lay crying in my bedroom curled in the fetal position on my bed, wrapped in the quilt I had taken home from the house trailer in Michigan. (Lauren had even sprayed it with her perfume for me.) When the phone rang again, it was Lauren.

"I'm not pregnant," she said. "I'm just late. And I have cramps now, so it's fine. I have to go. I don't want to talk anymore."

After that Lauren didn't return my calls for weeks. I became obsessed by the silence between the two of us, imagining that she was having sex with the boys from the baseball team, imagining her soft little body pressed up against the ones who called me a faggot, any one of them, or all of them at once.

It all seems dramatic now, looking back on it. But then it's funny the way things spiral out of control and become something real and not just sixteen and sentimental. The whole world can seem to break open into a weeping gouge. I remember grieving the breakup one evening in my basement bedroom. I couldn't get over it for weeks on end. My parents were upstairs, drinking too much wine, drunk with dinner guests. I could hear them through the chimney in the empty fireplace, saying last good-byes.

"It's time for us to go," I heard a man say.

"Go start the car, honey," I heard the man's wife say.

I heard the front door close.

"I'm going to use the bathroom," my mom said.

I heard my mother's feet pad up the stairs, which left the woman and my dad alone. It was quiet for several moments. Then I heard the sound of feet on the hardwood floor. Then I heard whispering.

Then lips smacking together. Intertwined. Sloppy.

Then another whisper.

"Thank you so much for having us."

"We should do this again soon," my dad replied, talking about more than just getting together with friends. The woman laughed.

Then I heard the door close, and it was quiet.

My mother's feet padded back down the stairs.

"Are they gone?"

In my memory everything changed after that night. I don't remember how it started or what I did next. I just remember a mood that came instantly, a haze that didn't leave until I couldn't remember I had ever felt anything different, until I was on my hands and knees in the jungle, vomiting, screaming, and purging my way back to that very night, that very moment at the chimney, listening to my father kiss another woman, and everything that followed, spilling out into a bucket.

Things like late-night Oldsmobile rides with white girls and boys who spoke like black people and wore saggy pants and sideways baseball hats. Crashing ghetto backyard cookouts with burnt hot dogs and rolling joints and big black women with breasts like watermelons and screaming babies. Just trying to get weed and get the hell out of there.

I remember beer cans and vomiting into the bushes, industrial parking lots and dime bags smacked with shitty seeds. Tongue-kissing girls with vodka on their breath, glittering fake eyelashes, and long fake nails, and then parents' empty houses that smelled like old smoke and ashtrays. Maybe a dad yelling at a flickering television set somewhere nearby, like a shadow dragon. Then reading my poetry notebook to stoned and drunk kids in bedrooms I didn't know, hearing them giggle and say, "Wow, that's some fucked-up shit." Or sometimes a fistfight would break out on the concrete, and people would gather around to watch it, like a band of vultures.

I remember pools of spattered blood and white-blue cop cars and breathalyzers and running through subdivisions to hide in alleyways and little patches of dead woodland between makeshift shitty parks with broken seesaws and rusted swing sets. And if I brought my guitar anywhere I'd be laid by some teenage girl who had sex with men twice my age.

She got on top of my legs and stomach. She rocked back and forth like I wasn't there. She looked at the ceiling and strangled out curses. I came in a few minutes but hid my orgasm so she wouldn't think I was a pussy, so she wouldn't realize that I came from a "preacher's" family, that I was a closet preppy and not eligible for true rebel status.

I had no curfew at home. In fact, most of the time, my family didn't know where I was. I would lie to them, or they might think, He's just down in the basement somewhere. . . .

"Son, we need to talk. Come into my study," my dad woke me from bed one morning. My eyes were bloodshot from pot and booze. I was slightly hungover and still stoned. I had gone to bed only an hour earlier. I was seventeen.

It was the first time I had entered my father's study in over a year. It looked the same, leathery and statuesque, but somehow plainer and dry around the edges, like a relic or museum artifact or old library book.

"Sit down, son," he said.

I sank into his armchair like it was a soft, leather glove. He sat across from me on a hard folding chair, like I was being interviewed. My mother stood by the door with her hand over her mouth, crying and looking off into space. I thought someone had died. I was waiting to hear who.

"Lauren's parents are leaving the church because Lauren says you raped her. They have a lawyer, and they are threatening to press charges." My father looked at me. It was quiet. I fought back tears. My voice shook. It had been over a year since I had lost my virginity.

"What?" I asked. "I haven't talked to Lauren for a long time."

"Did you have sex with her?"

"No," I said. "Never."

"You didn't have sex with her when you two were dating?" My dad looked deep into my eyes.

"We lost our virginity together," I said. "That's all. It's no big deal. Most of my friends have lost it."

"And she was okay with it?"

"What do you mean?"

"She says you raped her, son."

"I didn't rape her, so go ahead, let them press charges all they want. Fuck them. I didn't *fucking* do anything." Hearing the sound of the words "fuck" and "fucking" coming out of my mouth made tears bulge up. I tried to hold them in as long as possible.

"Tell us exactly what happened."

"Nothing happened," I said. "It's none of your business, especially if all you think is that I raped her."

And even after I told the story about losing my virginity in the house trailer and falling in love and the pregnancy test, my parents didn't fully trust me. I was carrying on about betrayal and the boys on the baseball team and hating the suburbs, licking my cotton lips because my mouth was dry from the marijuana.

"Are you high?" my mother finally asked, looking at my red eyes.

I hung my head and didn't answer.

Then my mother cried for much longer than I did, and my parents sent me to see another pastor friend, named Dale, for spiritual counseling.

Stoned for my meeting with Dale, I remember him doing most of the talking. Talking about how *his son hated him, too*.

"My son stole a car years ago," Dale said, as if admitting the largest secret of his life.

I stared at him.

"Your dad and I bailed him out of jail. I thought my son did it because of me, but then I realized that he's a grown man. You see, he made his decision and not me. That wasn't my failure as a father." Then finally he said, "You realize your parents love you?"

I thought to myself, *I am so high*.

Listening to Pastor Dale talk for only a short while, it dawned on me that Dale disliked my family. Dale had been a former superior of my father's in the Methodist conference. Now my father was his superior. Dale wasn't counseling me. I wasn't even there to Dale. Dale was somewhere else, talking to someone else. I realized that I didn't know whom Dale was talking to, not entirely, and I knew that Dale didn't realize he wasn't really talking to "me." I thought to myself, *Is this what it's like to be a shrink? I feel like Dale's shrink right now*.

"Your dad is a wonderful, wonderful man. I mean wonderful, Adam. Really wonderful. I'm glad he sent you to talk to me. Really glad. Tell me the truth. You can tell me everything. Man to man. Let's really get into it man to man. Your dad's not here. Sometimes men are too rough with women. It's in our nature. Your dad doesn't have to know what really happened. They're getting a lawyer anyhow. Nothing will happen to you. Your dad doesn't have to know a thing."

Dale's voice became a drone as he almost begged me to tell him I had done something wrong or that I disliked my father or that he had been a good father to *his* son. I thought to myself, *I wonder what would happen if everybody at church smoked pot on Sunday morning? Would they see what I'm seeing right now? See through the façade? Would it be a great big counseling session turned backward? Would they be singing to God, or would they be singing to something else? Were the people writing all those biblical psalms writing poetry to God, or was the poetry for someone else? Were my parents listening to me when I told them what happened with Lauren, or were they hearing someone else in their head? Is my dad in love with another woman or with something else? Are all of my sappy love poems actually for my soul mate, or are they for someone else? Was I dating Lauren or the idea of somebody I had made up in my head? Did I actually give my virginity away if the person I gave it to wasn't the person I thought she was? I feel so enlightened. Or maybe I'm just superhigh right now? I should talk to Dale more often!*

Digging under my bed the evening after I visited with Dale, smoking another joint, and paging through stacked journals of poetry and letters to my future wife, I found a handwritten note from Lauren. It was scribbled on the cover of a church bulletin.

I love the poem you wrote to me. I thought I would feel guilty losing my virginity, but I don't. I loved it. And I will love you always and forever! You're my soul mate. My one and only.

Yours, Lauren

Above her words was an illustration from the church bulletin of the Virgin Mary, looking like a sad phantom, holding the radiant virgin star of the sea in her hands, cupped between her cloaked hips. For a time it had felt as though I had actually committed the crime and raped my first sweetheart.

I stared at Lauren's letter for a long time, reading and rereading it. While I sat wondering what could have possessed Lauren to make up such a bold-faced lie, I became angrier and angrier with her, unconsciously letting my joint fall off from my lip. *Dumb fucking whore. That's all you ever were.* And by the time I realized the joint had fallen out of my mouth, the fiery cherry burned a hole in the carpet.

CHAPTER 19

SINS OF THE FATHERS (II)

The air was so silent that electrons might have been heard moving through the frozen January sky. An ice storm had silenced the streets and covered them with slick crystal. Flickering yellow lampposts were sparkling silver with atmospheric diamonds. The branches of the trees were breaking off everywhere, like stiff tentacles hanging heavy, like jagged thunderbolts waiting to fall and strike the earth. In warm living rooms, on television sets, the weatherman warned of a live power wire on Main Street in Manistee. The power company was on their way. It was 1964.

My father's father had been a chain smoker and a nasty drunk since returning home from the Korean War. Whenever my father heard his dad yelling at his mother, cursing and stumbling into the walls and breaking glass, he would go outside to play. So while his parents fought inside the house the night of the ice storm, and while he chewed on a snowball and peed in a snowbank in his backyard, my dad found something most peculiar. As he spelled his name in urine, his yellow stream found a strange object protruding from the bank. To him it looked like a small, brown glove sticking out of the snow. He looked closer and crouched down on his knees, his icy breath masking the object for a moment.

He touched the fingers of a brown hand the size of a baby's. It was frozen stiff. He held it for a moment in silence and then gently tugged on it, pulling it from the hard, icy tomb of the snowbank. Then his eyes grew as large as saucers, and the little boy jumped to his feet, gasping.

He stared at the face of a frozen, brown monkey with bared, yellow teeth.

"That's a frozen monkey!" the boy shouted out. He slipped on the ice and fell straight backward onto his back.

It was silent for a moment.

He looked around where he lay. He shouted again as though the monkey might attack him. "It's a monkey!"

Nobody answered. The frozen tree branches sounded like wind chimes and glass clinking together in the breeze and light rain. He looked around the empty streets and realized there was no one there to hear him. He looked again at the frozen monkey in the snowbank. He quickly reasoned with himself that the monkey could not possibly be thawed and kept as a pet, that it was dead specifically because it was frozen or had frozen because it was dead. Either way it wasn't coming back to life.

While he began to imagine science fiction possibilities, things like flashing red lights and cryogenic hibernation machines bringing the monkey back to life, strangely, he didn't stop to wonder why a monkey was in his wintry backyard in northern Michigan to begin with. Instead he felt quite at home with its presence and suddenly confident of its importance. It must mean something. An omen. A sign. He imagined that presenting it to his mother and father might stop their fighting.

Taking small steps, he walked carefully across the slippery hard surface of the snow back to the house, carrying the monkey by its tail. As he approached the spring-loaded back door of the house he could hear his father yelling. His knocking interrupted his father's fist shaking and glass breaking. Then he saw his mother through the window. She appeared in the jaundiced yellow light of the kitchen, one hand pointing at her husband with the Bible and the other hand on her hip.

Then she opened the screen door. "What do you want?" she snapped at the boy.

The little boy held the monkey in the air. "Look at what I found, Mom!"

"What is that?" his mother asked.

"Put it back where you found it," she said to my dad, quickly.

"But it's a monkey!" he replied. "Look at it."

"Here, let me see that." The boy held out the monkey for his mother to see. "I'm not touching that thing," she said. "Throw it back where you found it. It's probably someone's pet, and it's probably diseased." With that she closed the door in the boy's face.

The boy walked back through the snow, crying as he went, falling on the ice and stumbling to the bank where he had found the monkey. He said his good-bye between sniffles, suddenly sentimental and attached to the dead animal, like the monkey had been his pet long before it died.

I've been somewhat obsessed with the story about the monkey, since my dad first told it to me near a tepee fire during a Minnesota winter. I can't get the image out of my mind: my father, as a helpless little boy, driven from the warmth of his home environment and into the cold of winter, trying to solve his parents' marital quarrel by presenting them with a dead monkey from his frozen backyard. As an adult, whenever I've asked my father about why his parents fought so much or what they might have been fighting about on the night he found the monkey, he's told me, "Well, my dad was a mean drunk who had cheated on your grandmother, at some point, and your grandmother was an extremely religious woman. Who knows what they were fighting about. I didn't know anything about why they fought when I was a boy. I just wanted them to stop or wanted to get away from it all. That's why I went outside all the time, and that's how I got into Native American culture. It was in the air back then. At least that's how I remember it. It was scary to be at home for a lot of us kids. It was confusing. I'm sure the monkey that night was trying to escape, too. I'm sure it was somebody's pet. My dad ended up throwing it in the dumpster the next day."

I've imagined my father talking to the dead monkey that night before he put it back into the snowbank, saying something boyish like "I don't know what jungle you came from, but you sure got a long ways away from your home. . . ."

CHAPTER 20

THE CAVE OF THE APOCALYPSE

I would never find out what motivated my first love to accuse me of rape. After confronting Lauren's parents with a lawyer and her own handwritten letter, a letter that clearly indicated our sexual relationship had been consensual, Lauren's family backed off. My father invited me into his study for another talk.

"Lauren's family is going through a hard time right now," he said. "I can't say much more, but it's over now, so let's put it behind us. How about it?"

As a kind of make-up gift, my dad invited me to accompany him on a study tour for Christian ministers. I was eighteen. The tour followed the apostle Paul's travels around the islands of the eastern Mediterranean and Greece and Turkey, including a trip to the place the last biblical book, Revelation, was written, on the island of Patmos, at the cave of the Apocalypse.

"John had the vision right here," our tour guide said. "Most likely this is also where John died. The island of Patmos does not have a natural water source. Roman prisoners died of dehydration."

The cave was dark. Dozens of tall Roman candles burned in brass holders throughout the rocky ledges and cupboards. Our study group stood in silence, looking at the groove in the rock bed of the cave.

"So this is where John saw the vision of the end of the world," somebody said. "You know, if he was so busy having this 'vision,' and was nearly dead from dehydration, then how did he manage to write a whole book about it?"

"The vision was recorded by a fellow prisoner, a young man who transcribed the vision as John reported it," our tour guide answered.

I looked across the cave. Standing in one of the dark corners next to a rock-shelf filled with candles, my dad whispered to a tall woman. She had dark brown hair and dark brown skin. She smiled at him.

The tour guide pointed to a split in the rocks of the ceiling. "This split was probably caused by an earthquake. And we all know that John's vision at the beginning of the Book of Revelation started with an earthquake."

I could feel my innards shaking. I clenched my teeth and shot my father a dirty look. He didn't notice. He kept whispering to the woman. Several people in our group saw me and looked worried that something was wrong. He finally looked at me and said, "You okay, sport?"

I didn't answer.

"He goes to the Baptist church because he can't be seen at his dad's church anymore. He's thinks I'm too liberal." He smiled at me like he was telling a joke we both knew.

Later that night I swallowed a handful of nighttime cough medicine pills and fell asleep on the deck of the cruise ship, trying to make the time pass faster, but the sleep didn't last. When I woke up the ship was still sailing under the moon. I returned to my cabin to find that my father was missing. The white sheets were torn apart on his bed, and two empty crystal wineglasses sat on the bureau. The wineglasses were stained deep in the stems with crimson red. I left the cabin and walked to the night lounge. My father sat with a group of men and women drinking ouzo. The tall woman with brown hair and brown skin sat next to my father, touching my dad's arm when she laughed.

The day after visiting the cave of the Apocalypse we traveled on a bus from an ocean port to the small mountain city of Laodicea in modern-day Turkey. In the apocalyptic Book of Revelation, John addressed the people of Laodicea, saying, "You are neither hot nor cold but lukewarm, and the Lord spits you out." Oddly enough, in the city of Laodicea the water is in fact lukewarm. An elevated cold spring and hot spring from the north and south ends of Laodicea flow down into the aqueducts, comingling and creating lukewarm water throughout the city. I wondered if John knew this unique fact about Laodicea when he received his vision.

"What does it feel like to live a lukewarm life?" my father asked. He stood on the side of a hill outside Laodicea preaching a special guest sermon for our study group. It was Sunday morning. Gray clouds covered the sky, and little droplets fell here and there. In the distance the Taurus Mountains towered like an ice giant. A sheep herder walked with his flock across an opposing hillside. His herd bell rang softly over the valley, and a dog followed him over the hills.

"John was speaking about hypocrisy," my dad said. Then he paused and looked for a moment as if he might cry. He got a lump in his throat and licked his lips. "But there is nothing more hypocritical than not being true to your self."

When we got home his adultery was more obvious.

"I'm going to get supplies," my dad said. "When I get home I will teach you how to change the oil in your car."

After three hours of waiting I drove to the house of the woman I suspected was his mistress, still hoping I might be wrong. His white Jeep Wrangler, adorned with Grateful Dead stickers, sat parked in her driveway.

I tried to expose my father's affair to my mother. I held a bottle of Zoloft in my hand, demanding answers.

"Oh, sweetie. He only takes them because he is overwhelmed by this church," my mom said.

"You don't believe me?" I asked. "These are proof that he doesn't like his life. He doesn't like us anymore, either. I'm telling you, he's having an affair."

"He's been on them for years. He just hasn't told you. Some

things are private. You know, just because you heard some silly things through the chimney or saw some suspicious things on a cruise ship, it doesn't mean your dad is guilty of a crime."

"I can't believe you don't believe me."

"Your father rebelled against his father, too. It's natural for fathers and sons to be competitive. And while we're on it, I want to tell you that it's embarrassing for this whole family that you attend the Baptist church," my mother said. "It doesn't look good that you're a Pentecostal. It makes us look like we don't have our son's best interests in mind. And you know we would die for you, don't you? We had a lawyer ready to defend you with that whole Lauren mess. Did you know that?"

One evening my dad came home drunk from his mistress's house when nobody was home but me. My mother and sister were away doing volcano relief work on the island of Monserrat. I heard my father vomiting in the bathroom. I helped him into his bed.

"It's no good," he said to me. His breath smelled like alcohol and undigested food.

"What's no good?" I asked. I fantasized my father would admit the affair.

"I shouldn't drink like this. I'm a little depressed is all."

"You sure that's it?" I asked.

Once he had fallen asleep I drank half a bottle of scotch from his private study. The next morning he made an out-of-the-ordinary visit to my basement bedroom. I was still sleeping and hungover from the scotch. It was a Saturday morning. Full of energy, he turned on my bedside lamp. I felt like I might vomit.

"I'm going to move the family to Michigan after you graduate this spring. Start over. I think it will be good for everybody. There are many good universities in Michigan. I can help you look if you want. I wanted to say thank you for helping me last night. I'm not going to drink any longer. It's making me depressed. It makes me feel like my dad used to be, you know? Well, you don't need to hear about that. But I really think you'll like Michigan," he said.

"Do what you need to do," I said.

"Are we okay? You and me? I was in rough shape last night. Thank you for helping me."

"Sure, Dad. We're fine."

"Would you like to move to Michigan?"

"What do you think?" I answered.

"We can talk about it," he said. "Grandma's health isn't so good. She and your grandpa would like us around. Your mom and I were sweethearts in Michigan. We grew up in Michigan. There's something about being home, you know? We can talk about it. I don't like it here, to be honest, and I think we could all use a change of scenery."

"Okay, Dad," I said. "Whatever."

"We could use the tepee again," he added. "We could put it up in the back forty acres of Grandpa's land. You would like that, wouldn't you?"

"Whatever," I said again.

"Your breath smells like alcohol. Were you drinking my liquor?"

"You have no room to talk," I said. "Just leave me alone."

While I was still attending the youth rallies and Pentecostal worship services at the Baptist church across town, my peers and youth ministers had something to say when I broke down during a Bible study about my father's affair, about how I'd been smoking pot and drinking, and about how I'd lost my virginity with Lauren and then slept around with random girls at parties.

"None of this is your fault," one pastor told me. "You're only behaving this way because your parents are not real Christians. You wouldn't be smoking dope or cigarettes or drinking booze and having sex if your parents were right with God. You know, young man, there was a fellow who wanted to follow Jesus, and he complained to Jesus that he had to bury his father first or his family would get angry with him. And do you know what Jesus told the man? He said to let the dead bury the dead. He told him to move on. Get to salvation or get out of the way. Now, it sounds to me like your father is *spiritually dead*, and the Lord is asking you to leave him behind. Your real father is the *heavenly father*, and he knows when you are troubled. Ask him to be your new family. Don't think twice about leaving home, son."

My breakdown at the youth group earned me a new girlfriend named Stephanie. Before she began dating me, Stephanie's family had said she was only allowed to date "Jesus." And when her parents finally let her date *me* it was only a short time before they said the same thing the Baptist youth pastor had told me.

"Follow Jesus, and he will give you a brand-new family and a brand-new life. So many of our youth group members are kids like you, whose parents believe in all kinds of sinful things. Homosexuality. Abortion. Evolution. The end times are coming, and it's a sign when children have to be more Christlike than their parents. We have outreach programs in the high schools for kids like you, to help you minister to your family. It's amazing our Stephanie found you and helped bring you back to God."

"Let them go to Michigan," Stephanie would say to me. For the rest of my senior year of high school, as my family prepared to move once again, she would say to me, "Come to college with me at Bethel. Stay here. Let them go. Bethel is a Baptist training school for men and women of God."

CHAPTER 21

○──────────○

A LIGHT IN THE DARK

When my fifteenth ceremony started, over two years since my very first cup, I was sitting upright in a chair. Domingo handed me a full cup of ayahuasca. I saw people receive that much ayahuasca before without anything extraordinary happening (for a ceremony). I hoped for the best.

"*Salud,*" I said. "*Salud,*" everybody in the mesa echoed.

I took five big gulps of the earthy brown liquid. I scowled. Outside, the jungle noises grew louder.

Within ten minutes the ceiling of the mesa had opened to blackness. The lodge spun upside down. I looked into a void below me. I dangled from the arms of my rocking chair, which had also turned upside down. In the shadows below I could see the flickering of fiery torches cascading orange light across stalagmites. Red colors emanated from the void, crawling upward to find me like serpents woven into evil mandalas.

"Everybody ready for a strong ceremony?"

I heard Ethan just starting the ceremony after the last cup had been administered back in the mesa, and while they were still sober people continued talking to one another. Then I heard the last physical echo of my fingers on the bindings of my rocking chair, losing their grip string by string, finger by finger.

The sound of a spinning plate yawned past my ears and collapsed on itself. I saw a squadron of foreign objects flying through my body, like UFOs. I felt evil shapes and laughter coursing through my bloodstream. Vines grew out of my orifices and wrapped around my throat, strangling me. A creature with reptilian eyes and barbed spiked dreadlocks crept up behind my shoulders and then peered around my neck and looked into my eyes. Its dripping wet claws dug into my ears. I was certain I had been given too much ayahuasca.

Oh, Jesus, I thought to myself. *I'm fucked.*

My limbs and joints moved up and down, clicking and clacking out of control. Snakes and spiders crawled into my body. The effects of the ayahuasca were stronger than ever before, and the intensity of the visions and level of my fear faster and more cunning than I had ever faced. I ground my teeth together and then fell out of my rocking chair and onto the floor of the mesa. I heard Ethan's voice saying, "Because you're ready for it."

I saw my father's face and his father's face, and then chieftains wearing skeleton masks in a row next to a stone gateway covered in black runes. One of the chieftains opened the door, and I looked into a black void. Then I was shaking on the floorboards as though I had undergone electroshock. The speed of my seizure grew. I saw millions of minuscule strings vibrating at light speed through my nervous system, until my body did not feel human any longer, pounds of flesh animated only by electricity, but I still shook. For one small moment it felt wonderful. I remember thinking, *Something miraculous is happening to me.*

But then somebody cried out, "He's having a seizure! He's on the floor right here in front of me, and I think he's having a seizure. Somebody do something!" Then I remember Ethan answering calmly, "This is normal, everybody. He will be okay. He's just purging. Let's get some water on him. Juan! *Agua, por favor.*"

Then I thought to myself, *I could be having a bad reaction. Is my heart beating?*

"Help, help, help, help, help," I screamed.

Then I lost the ability to speak. Water was poured onto my body. I woke throwing myself into a wall. Large hands wrapped around my shoulders. Then black again. Shaking. Screaming. Black. I tore off my clothing. Limp while somebody walked me to the shower again, this time naked.

"Adam. Turn to Jesus, Adam. Focus on the love in your heart. You have to believe in yourself," Ethan said.

"But, but, but, but, but," I said.

"No more buts," Ethan said. He was holding my hand.

"Can I touch your face?" I asked him.

"No," Ethan said.

"Where am I?"

I wandered through golden cities in the desert, all flames and tall shadows covering the tops of forever temples like a sinister fog, shadow bats chasing me through empty city streets. Didn't know where I was, but knew I was somewhere. Screaming so hard the golden sand would light up like blood beneath my feet, and I would find myself snapping my jaw back and forth in the mesa, digging my fingernails into the floorboards, disoriented and begging, water being poured over my head.

"You're in the shower," Ethan said. I heard the hissing sound of the spigot above me. Cold piercing bullets of water sucked at me like black holes, pulling me out of my body through the stone tiles. I stumbled out of the shower and fell onto the ground. Black again. I lay on my back laughing out of control, dark laughter, funny laughter, angry laughter. Juan pulled my soggy sweat pants up my legs and then wrapped me in a blanket.

"I'm freezing," I said.

I could not hold on to objects or possessions. I could not hold on to religion or clothing. I could not hold on to success or health. I could not hold on to a body or mind.

"I'm the king of bullshit," I yelped with delight. I had the urge to dig feces out of myself and spread it everywhere, but Ethan's hands held mine firmly.

"We are not going to baby you," Ethan said. "When you spent all that time condemning others with the Bible, blaming your mother and father for your unhappiness, you created your own private hell. Now you're cleaning yourself up. You're releasing all the blame and judgment." For the first time in hours I heard other people in the mesa vomiting, and I remembered the ayahuasca ceremony happening around me. Then it was gone again.

I saw the designs of fear. Primitive temples made for human sacrifice. I saw possession in the kings of Egypt. I saw possession in the priest castes of the Mayas and Hindus. I saw men in dark robes with their eyes rolled back in their heads, seizing from the mouth. I saw the alien abduction of the mind. The obsession with an unknown, unforeseen invading species. The idea that something we cannot see can do something to us we cannot see coming. Flying saucers zipped through the trees, and schizophrenics and lepers hung upside down from the metal branches of buildings and city skyscrapers. I saw metal rods and iron limbs. I saw robotic armies of Zen-perfect anger. Razor-sharp evil. Then crop circles rising out of the ground and briefcase bombs annihilating New York City. Men on top of horned beasts rode through a lost civilization, wandering past money changers and smoke and belly dancers. The Wall Street, back-alley crapshoot of some ancient market. The archetypes of the old were the same as those of the new. Their designs the stuff of dark magic.

"We're all going to die in 2012. I've been reading about it," I whimpered between tears.

"It's best to stay away from doomsday predictions," Ethan said. "It sometimes hurts to heal, and that might be the case for human beings, but the light is always stronger than the darkness, and everything will be mended eventually. Everybody loves big drama, but it makes a lot more sense to be gentle and kind to each other. That way we don't have to create a big mess, or the Apocalypse. There's an easier way and a burden far lighter to shoulder. So in the future you'll know how to forgive yourself and others so you don't have to face your own personal apocalypse when you drink ayahuasca."

"I only wanted to fit in," I said, referring to so many different things I was both seeing and feeling at once. "I just wanted friends. I just wanted to be loved."

"That might be true. But good friends don't demand love, and they don't take it from others or blame people from whom they aren't getting what they want. Entire religions and empires have been built on the premise that there are not enough resources to go around and that we have to compete with each other or take things by force in order to be happy. The only reason anybody ever lusts after power is because they are afraid of love. That fear is what you are here to face. And when you face it, you will meet the best friend of your life. You will meet God. And your truest self. You will see yourself clearly for the first time, and then you will start making the kind of friends and feeling the love you've wanted for so long. You will find your destiny. But first you have to believe in your heart that love exists within you, and you have to face every fear that says otherwise. This is what *spiritual practice* is all about. When we allow the fear of love to dominate our lives, we get sick. So when you drink ayahuasca medicine, you face whatever fears of love you have, and you feel better. You feel love again.

As the ceremony progressed I found myself back in the mesa at the same spot, sitting on the floor near the shower stall. My body was slowly gaining control again. I lay on my back while leftover tremors shook through my legs.

The more I had cried out for help and mercy, the more I understood something was surviving, something whose design was not of my own making and whose existence transcended characterization or effort, even pain and suffering. My heart was still beating. The air was coming in and out of my lungs, and I was still alive. As I survived more of the night, inch by inch, I was aware of a life force beyond and behind each word I could use to describe it: a light in the midst of darkness. My life had never been judged but always sustained by the luminescent beating of something called my heart.

"I have a heart," I said between tears. "It's never given up on me."

"Never," Ethan echoed immediately. "Never."

"It's not just the heart in my chest," I said.

"It's so much more," Ethan called back.

"I'm still here," I said.

"Where else could you be?" Ethan replied.

"I believe in myself."

"Now you're talking." A few people in the mesa clapped and cheered for me.

"This medicine is kicking my ass," I said.

"It's not a punishment," Ethan said. "It's your heart opening. You chose it because you are brave. It hurts at first."

"It's so real."

"For the first time in the past four hours, you're starting to make sense."

Ethan laughed from all the way down in his stomach.

"Seriously," he said. Then I laughed with him, and the entire mesa clapped and joined together to celebrate the opening of my heart.

CHAPTER 22

A KINGDOM DIVIDED
AGAINST ITSELF

Central to the Christian Gospel story is the death and resurrection of Jesus. The unjust murdering of a loving prophet, his full acceptance of and surrender to death, and the resurrection of Christ and subsequent Pentecost: the birth of Jesus' Holy Spirit that would remain on earth with mankind. But if the story had ended there, then the Holy Spirit would have restored balance by now, and our planet would be living in harmony. Since this is not the case, it is natural to ask when the full atonement and establishment of heaven on earth will happen. Can it actually happen? Is it going to happen soon?

Since the earliest decades and centuries after the death and resurrection of Christ, Christians have turned to the visions of St. John of Patmos, the writer of the Book of Revelation, for answers about the end times. In his apocalyptic narrative of the end of time, St. John wrote about a great time of tribulation for the kingdoms of earth, at which point a second Christ would come to fight an evil beast and by doing so establish a New Jerusalem. Although scholars have debated the symbolic nature of the Book of Revelation ever since it was written, the promise of a second coming of Christ was first spoken of by Jesus himself. Later, almost every single writer of the New Testament would share the same prophetic vision of a second coming of Christ.

After communicating with Jesus in ayahuasca visions I feel more like a Christian now than ever before. It's just that my idea of what it means to be a Christian has become something beyond the doctrine or dogma of a church, more than the observations or interpretations of scholars over the centuries. Like the people who lived before Jesus, who had no knowledge of his human person yet but must have had access to the holy doctrine Jesus incarnated, so, too, must people today get in touch with the holy doctrine of the Christ in a form different from the historical person of Jesus. Especially if we are to understand what the "second coming" of Christ might look like.

After all, the holy doctrine of Jesus was not the exclusive property of Jesus. Rather, it was Jesus' calling to replant the holy doctrine in the form of his life and his ministry on earth. The holy doctrine has always been the property of God. Since the message of redemption and harmony has always been for the benefit of the entire planet, we have to look carefully at the person of Jesus and his situation in history to discover why so much emphasis has been placed on Jesus' name. It is our duty to do this since Jesus himself never would have advocated religious wars or hatred in his name. And it is also our duty to do this since Jesus was, without doubt, a very special prophet, very different from the others who had come before him.

Seeing a more holistic vision of the life of Jesus, we might start by envisioning his place in the physical ecology of the planet. The desert of the Middle East, an area more densely populated by alpha-male species than perhaps anywhere else on earth. Dry. Barren. Difficult to survive. Lacking water (a universal symbol of the feminine). It is safe to say that Jesus was born at the epicenter of a kind of human virus that was beginning to spread across the planet in the forms of the Western expansion, colonialism, Christian-Muslim extremism, imperialism, and later scientific materialism. And has there been any force more dominant, competitive, and violent than the force of Western, alpha-male, secular-materialistic, market-centered kingdoms?

As we watch our "mother earth" suffer the blows of this masculine-heavy force more and more every day, we will be faced with a choice. Against a force so single-minded and aggressive in its quest for power, how can those of us who want peace and harmony choose to be anything but united, within ourselves and with each other?

Of course, it is often at this point in the conversation that many spiritual people will say there is no need for urgency or the uniting of our "effort" to accomplish anything at all. All suffering or imbalance is said to be an illusion of the ego. Violence and chaos are part of change, and change is simply the nature of reality. Everything is already perfect. We can turn inward and transcend the illusion that there is any conflict, or ever has been, and then wake up to the complete and perfect oneness of all reality.

Most of the time this "turning inward" is prescribed through various ascetic practices. These strict practices have seemed to me mostly antisocial and impersonal. They tend to emphasize the idea that both dualism and individuality are by nature painful or fallen states of being. The emphasis is placed on the impersonal quest for the transcendence of pain and dualism rather than on a personal and socially active paradigm of compassion and healing. In the former paradigm, all storylines are an illusion of a reality whose fundamental nature is fear and death. In the latter, unavoidable evolution is the redemptive story of God's personal creation, whose true nature is love and light. Any vessel that carries this redemptive story to our planet is hence considered an "anointed one," a messiah. Jesus happened to be an incredibly powerful messiah, an evolutionary catalyst for God's works on this planet.

Through many ayahuasca visions, I have asked questions about the second coming. How can I understand what my role is? What is the second coming? Is it real? The answer I have received from Jesus, in each and every vision, has been the same. The second coming *is* real. It is the emergence of a united force of a transformative culture aimed at the construction of a more loving, more harmonious planet. A storyline of inevitable redemption. A storyline that, at this moment in history, asks us to believe in evolution and to work for the good rather than attempt to simply transcend the "illusion" of pain and material reality.

Ayahuasca's role in this storyline seems to be a special one. In the brew of ayahuasca, a new kind of sacrament is revealed. A holy healing technology that can transform the powers of chaos and darkness into light. The leaf (a feminine symbol) and the vine (a masculine symbol) come together to open a visible porthole to a spiritual dimension of life that exists whether we believe it or not. Within that spiritual realm the same redemptive, evolutionary storyline is playing out. And it turns out we are not alone on this planet, or in this universe. More like fish swimming in a liquid filled with spiritual beings, we are just beginning to recognize, just learning to see, who is swimming all around us. The very emergence of this spiritual reality, not even touching on the storylines also happening in these realms, will greatly change human consciousness as more people witness it firsthand.

Once people are exposed to the spiritual realm, the next step they will need to take is to connect to the Christ consciousness within it, the holy spirit of God's evolutionary work in creation. As this happens, one time will end and a new one will begin. One era of human consciousness will be born as something new. And while some may initially choose to ignore the spiritual reality emerging, eventually every knee will bow and every tongue proclaim that universal love is our King and Queen. Our God. Our Mother and our Father. Our Gospel.

CHAPTER 23

CLIMBING JACOB'S LADDER

After graduating from high school, angry with my father and mother, I decided to attend college with Stephanie at Bethel and stay in St. Paul while my family moved to Michigan to yet another Methodist church. In the Old Testament the Hebrew word "Bethel" most closely means "House of God." The village of Bethel, thought to be just north of the city of Jerusalem, was said to be the place where Jacob, the grandson of Abraham, fell asleep on a large rock and received the vision of a ladder stretching into the heavens, connecting the divine realms to the earth. In the dream at Bethel God said to Jacob, "I am with you wherever you go, and I will watch over you."

Before moving into my college dormitory in the fall, I landed a summer job house-sitting for a Baptist missionary named Richard.

I was nineteen. Rich lived in the suburbs, and every summer while he traveled overseas into the mission fields, his wife, Beth, stayed at home to water the plants and walk the dog. Tragically, while attending her first mission trip with Rich in Central America, Beth suffered a sudden heart attack and died in their tent while sleeping. Determined to continue his summer mission trips in memory of his wife and out of duty to the Lord, Rich needed a house sitter to water Beth's plants and walk the family dog. One evening after a worship service, a youth minister at the Baptist church recommended me.

"He's leaving his family to attend Bethel. His parents are not men and women of God. This is a big leap of faith for Adam. I think he would make an ideal person to watch your house this summer, Rich."

I remember the summer at Richard's house, vividly. It was hot, and I felt in between worlds. The tall brown fence enclosing the luscious green backyard. Mowing the lawn between rain storms. Smoking joints and cigarettes under the moonlight. A big oak tree with branches hanging over the top of the house. The way the branches would fan the deck with water when it rained. The rusty basketball hoop in the front driveway, young couples walking babies in strollers or workmen on tarred rooftops with shingles and nail guns, the sounds of barking dogs.

The only news I got from Michigan was my mother's occasional phone calls. She would phone to talk about my dad's health or worry about mine.

"Your father is sick. He switched antidepressants, so that could be the culprit. But he's not sleeping well, and he's crying a lot for no reason, and he doesn't want to work in the new church very much.

It's too stressful. He's burnt out. He falls asleep in the shower. It's too much. How are you doing? Do you need grocery money? Are you okay on your own? Okay. Okay. I'm sorry. I'm just tired. We miss you. It doesn't feel right without you hanging around in the basement. There is a basement in this house, too. You know you're welcome to come home for the summer before school starts. But you don't want to be home anymore; I understand."

The only serious problem with living in Rich's house was dealing with his ferocious dog. It took half the summer for me to befriend Laser, his large and growly German shepherd. Laser flunked out of police dog training as a young adult, and when I arrived at Rich's house, Laser stood at the top of the stairwell growling at me. Each night after that, a stare down reminiscent of the whistling theme song to *The Good the Bad and the Ugly* took place, and each night Laser won by forcing me to sprint into the basement as fast as I could, slamming the door behind me, his paws thudding and scratching, his dog voice barking, "I will eat you alive!"

The only way to approach Laser was with dog treats from the pantry. At the sight of a treat, Laser's ferocity transformed into childlike innocence. "Follow me, psycho," I said, leading Laser with a milk bone to his water dish.

Upon leaving for the mission field, Rich had said something peculiar about Laser and the spirit of his dead wife, Beth. Something that struck me as particularly "off" for a staunch, fundamentalist Christian.

"My wife's ghost is still in the house. Laser is very protective of her presence. He won't let you upstairs unless you announce yourself to Beth or carry a milk bone. She stands at the top of the stairs with him just like she used to every night when I came home. You'll feel her. Do you know what the name Beth means? It means the abiding place of God. She is still here all of the time. She waits for me at night."

It hadn't occurred to me that Rich could have been serious until one night upon my race to the basement Laser managed to snag my arm and break the skin. While bandaging my bloody arm, I thought to myself, *This will end with my death or his. I will beseech the spirit of Beth for help.*

It had been a long time since I considered the existence of ghosts and spirits, as far back as my childhood, but as Rich spoke so fervently about Beth and because I was speaking in tongues on a regular basis at the Baptist church anyway, I reasoned that it might work to introduce myself to the spirit of his dead wife.

The next evening when I returned home, Laser growled at me as usual. This time I carried a lit joint in my hand, smoking to relax myself. Laser's teeth were bared, and he was crouched and ready to spring at me from the top of the stairs. I closed my eyes.

"Beth," I said, "I'm here to say hello and ask if you can help Laser calm down. I believe this house is big enough for all of us."

It's true that I felt silly talking out loud to a Baptist missionary's dead wife's ghost and an angry German shepherd standing at the top of a stairwell waiting to eat me, but then something happened that changed the course of my summer: Laser turned his head to the side the way dogs do and looked at me with a puzzling grin. Then he made a small and playful bark and his tail began to wag back and forth.

I looked at the joint between my fingers. Laser watched it carefully. The smoke twisted and curled into the air. "You want some *pot?*" I asked, dumbfounded. He cocked his head to the side again.

"Are you serious?"

Laser barked.

"No way," I said.

Laser barked again.

"Unbelievable. All right, but you get no pot if you bite. This joint will be all mine. You got that?"

And that was how the friendship started. Although it wasn't until halfway through the summer, it began by me leading Laser onto the porch like the joint was a milk bone. Then, sitting under the moonlight, I shared a small bowl of potato chips and blew the occasional long streams of smoke into Laser's face. Laser responded by licking the smoke and chasing it with his snout, and then eating potato chips and falling asleep at my feet.

After that, each night I came home Laser no longer waited at the top of the stairwell. I found him instead lying on the couch (which he was not allowed on) or resting peacefully somewhere snoring, waiting for me to rub his belly.

Before I left Rich's to move to my college dormitory at Bethel, I locked the house and watered Beth's plants one last time. I said good-bye to Laser, and I could almost hear Beth's voice, somewhere far away, saying "thank you."

When Rich returned home from the mission field, the very day I moved into Bethel, he called on the telephone and said, "I want to say sorry for spooking you about Beth. I think she's with God in heaven, not hanging around here like a ghost. She was a strong Christian. A real woman of God. She's with the Father now. No more silly *ghost in the house* business. It would be nice to think that way, I admit. You know, I think Laser must finally know that she's gone because he doesn't wait at the top of the stairs anymore. He just lies out in the sun all afternoon. Or climb onto the couch. Very strange for him to be so relaxed. You must have had a calming effect on him."

"You never know," I said.

At Bethel, the halls were filled with athletic guys twice my size, everyone calling himself a man of God. They were the sons and daughters of wealthy Republicans and urban fundamentalists. They carried Bibles and drove sports cars. They wore name-brand clothing and attended nightly study groups with titles like "Godly Money Management," "How to Date Jesus," and "Healing Homosexuals." My resident advisor wrote me up for burning incense the first weeks of school. "We can't have a fire in the dorm," he said. "And incense doesn't set a good example because it smells like marijuana."

Regardless of the fact that I had been burning incense in order to *cover up* the smell of marijuana, it struck me as funny that my resident advisor was opposed to incense solely on the basis of its olfactory association *to* marijuana. (Forget that I had a bag of weed in my desk drawer; patchouli was guilt by association!)

But his naiveté inspired me. I snuck out of the dormitory at night to smoke pot on the rooftop, and sometimes one of my hall mates, whom I quickly converted into a pot smoker, joined me and we broke into the football stadium to smoke grass on the fifty-yard line. Not only did I realize right off the bat that I was at Christian bootcamp college, but my Baptist girlfriend was instantly impressed with the wealthy "men of God" who roamed the hallways and led candlelight worship services in their bedrooms with guitars on their laps, surrounded by flocks of wooing college girls. The "men of God" gazed into the candlelight after singing each worship song for the ladies, saying, "God is good."

A common meme on the campus of Bethel that every freshman guy talked about was the motto "A ring by spring." Everybody knew that most women of Bethel were not looking for a job or a career.

That was seldom. It was far more common for women attending Bethel to seek their MRS degree. My Baptist high school sweetheart was one such woman. Intimidated by her attraction to the jocular "men of God," I decided to join the club lacrosse team. I feared I was effeminate, overly sensitive. When such fears persist, what else can a young man do but play a full-contact sport?

One Sunday afternoon I joined a group of guys from the lacrosse team for a game of tackle football on the men's practice field. For the first time since living in the small town of Cambridge, I felt as though I belonged somewhere. There was a spirit in the air at Bethel. I was part of something again. I attended all of the Bible and lifestyle study groups. For each lap I ran around the track with my lacrosse stick, I thought to myself: *Now you're doing it. You've gotta stop smoking grass and drinking and breaking all the rules. You've gotta read your Bible more often. You've gotta be tough.*

"Go deep!" the quarterback called out.

"I'm open!" I yelled.

I remember it was overcast and windy. October. I was wearing a white T-shirt and wind pants. The ground was hard and cold. I lifted my hand in the air. I saw the brown leather pig skin spiraling through the empty atmosphere. I caught the ball and trotted into the end zone.

I pushed people and brushed shoulders. We fell onto the ground in piles and laughter. All afternoon we played.

"I've got him!" I called out.

One heavyset guy ran toward me in the open field. He carried the football, tucked beneath his right arm. His left arm stuck straight out to block my tackle. I grabbed at his chest but tripped and fell. On my way down I undercut his body at the knees. We spun together in a whirlwind and crashed. My left elbow planted first. His body followed closely behind on top of my left shoulder, like a sledgehammer pounding a tent stake into the ground. I screamed.

"My arm is broken!"

Then in my memory it was quiet. The clouds were suddenly gone. I couldn't feel anything, as if I were dreaming, looking into the white.

"He's in shock," somebody said. "Don't move him. Call nine-one-one!"

I screamed again. Then I mumbled, "I want to play lacrosse. I want to be on the team. Goddamn it."

The weight of my body was splinting my broken humerus into the ground. I could not see the break but knew that my bone had penetrated the skin. My legs shook uncontrollably, and my eyes rolled back into my head. The other guys on the field stood fifteen feet away from me. Somebody sprinted back to the dormitory to phone the ambulance.

"Let's pray," somebody said. They got in a circle of fifteen and prayed for me. I could feel they were afraid, and it scared me even more. I felt my bone digging through my left arm and into the mud.

I remember the ride to the hospital like it was only one turn of a siren and back. I talked to the paramedic.

"I don't think I would care about clothing so much if I had your job. Always cutting people's shirts off at the scene of the accident. Did you cut my shirt off?"

"Yes, we cut it off," the paramedic laughed at me.

"I thought so," I said. I passed out again.

When the paramedics flipped my body over on the field, my left biceps had curled into a rainbow and my upper arm was no longer straight but in a tight knot of muscle. The bone pushed barely up and out through the skin. There was blood. I remember a paramedic injecting me several times with morphine and saying, "You won't feel a thing. There, there."

I sat on the emergency room table for twelve hours with my open arm in a splint, waiting for surgery. I passed out from the pain several times. My family was in Michigan, two states and a Great Lake away from me. Stephanie sat next to me and kept saying, "You shouldn't have been so rough out there. A man of God has to know his limits, cute stuff."

"It was just a game," I said. "I'm not a pussy."

When I woke the next morning after surgery I was in a hospital bed. The room was white and blue and green. Stephanie watched the television. It was dark outside. She fed me through a straw, and then a surgeon spoke to me. "The good news is that we repaired the bone in your arm with a permanent plate and seven screws. So you won't have to wear a cast for long. But the bad news is that your radial nerve was stretched and your left hand is paralyzed. A stretch is not as bad as a tear. Stretches can heal with physical therapy."

When my parents arrived at the hospital they were happy to see me. We had not seen each other since they had moved to Michigan and since I had moved into Rich's house after graduating from high school. My mother hugged me and explained to me the different parts of my arm, the nerves and tissues, the bones and ligaments. She sat next to my hospital bed, reassuring me. "We'll need to find you a ride to physical therapy. They can do wonders nowadays. You will get that hand back in no time."

It was also the first time I spoke to my father in months. I heard about his changes in medication, his tears, and his growing desire to leave church work, only through my mother's telephone calls. Each time I had wanted to say, "He's feeling guilty about the affair, that's all," but I held back. I wondered from time to time if guilt and shame could kill a person. I hoped my father would tell the truth for his own sake.

In the hospital room, on my third and final day in bed, my dad helped me rise in the morning. He helped me walk to the bathroom. One hand underneath each armpit. The sun was so brand-new that my eyes hurt, and my feet felt weak and heavy, like anchors. My head spun, and I almost fell while I tried to urinate, but my father caught me. When I couldn't urinate he called for the nurse. She inserted a catheter. I cried out of embarrassment. I did not want him there to witness a tube being inserted into my urethra, but there he was. He looked out the window at the sun. He didn't say anything much. Just held my hand and squeezed.

"How you feeling, sport?"

I began to cry.

"I hope I can move my hand again someday," I said.

"You will," he said. "I know you will."

Then he brought a bowl of warm, soapy water next to my bed and lathered my face with shaving cream. Small stroke by gentle drag, he shaved my face.

"I didn't realize you grew a beard so fast," he said. "Seems like you were a little boy just the other day."

I remember the sunlight and the warm, thick sound of the hot razor pulling gently across the stubbles of hair on my face, on my cheeks, on my chin, and in the grooves beneath my jaw. I remember the clack of the blade on the edge of the porcelain bowl when he cleaned the razor, and I remember that it was quiet except for the faint beep of a cardiac machine at the other end of the room, separated only by a thin, white curtain. Someone much older than I and nearer to death, an elderly man suffering from something I did not know, was only several feet away. I could hear him breathing. The rising. The sinking. I didn't need an apology from my dad that morning. I didn't have any questions, and I didn't need any answers. It was enough that he sat next to me.

When I returned to life at Bethel everything was different. I implored the student association to help me find a car or bus so that I could see my physical therapist. My left hand was paralyzed. I spoke to a secretary who said, "We have no services available for someone in your situation. You are responsible for your own health care needs."

My mother telephoned the college. "We're hundreds of miles away from our son. Surely you have out-of-state students who need help getting medical treatment. And whatever happened to this college being a Christian community? Can't you help us? Our son's hand is paralyzed. You are supposed to be full of good resources. We're paying for him to be in school and going into debt to do so."

Reluctantly, an upperclassman from one of my Bible studies (upperclassmen were allowed to have cars) agreed to drive me to the physical therapist once a week, but it was clear my injury and need for medical attention was a nuisance to the image and lifestyle of the campus.

As the semesters at Bethel passed and the rehabilitation of my paralyzed hand progressed rather slowly, I withdrew from Bethel's

Christian social life and invested myself in my studies. I took extra philosophy and theology courses, starting with classical Greek philosophy and mythology. Dismissing my theology textbooks in favor of the secular classics (which were mostly observed from a safe and "historical" distance), I worked from Homer to Plato and Aristotle, reading my way through Greek and Western history until reaching more modern writers like Kant, Hegel, Descartes, and Mills. Then contemplating existential writers like Sartre and darker subjects, like being and nothingness. Then Derrida, Emily Dickinson, and William Blake. Darwin and Jung. Freud and Ezra Pound. Marijuana was a constant source of solitary comfort and guidance, and my exploration of thinkers was reinforced by the lyrics and melodies of singers saying the same things in harmonic musical structures: The Moody Blues, The Replacements, Radiohead, Neil Young, and The Smashing Pumpkins.

Sitting on top of my dormitory roof one night during the winter months of study, I made snow angels on my back while listening to my headphones and smoking a pipe filled with cannabis. When I stood up and looked at my angelic creations under the light of the Minnesota moon, long swiping arms like butterfly wings and the dress of my legs, like Leonardo da Vinci's naked man covered in sparkling frost, I saw the creative expressions of my physical body, the way each building, classroom, and bedroom on campus seemed like a convalescence of geometric shapes and possibilities.

I attended Pentecostal worship services on Sunday nights in the Benson Great Hall, stoned and red eyed. My worship experiences were more interesting than ever before. I noticed that certain faces in the ocean of worshippers were insane, faces lost in emotions and lifting grateful hands up to the heavens. Others gyrated in angry fits. Some faces were self-righteous and arrogant, some pious. Sermons veered off course into matters of despair and anger, although the actual words of the sermon were of peace and Jesus. I heard things hidden behind words, and I thought to myself, *Are these details there all of the time? What are we worshipping?* It was all something called "being in the spirit."

I tried to share my worship observations with a roommate.

"Those worship services aren't exactly what people think they are," I said. "I can feel it when I'm stoned, but I'm not sure how to explain it. I think people are in the spirit world at the worship services, but I think some of the spirits they are hanging out with aren't actually Christian."

"I think it's great you're going back to worship service," he answered. "I thought you were dropping off the face of the earth for a while. I'm glad to see God called you back home. But why are you still smoking pot?"

"I don't think I was ever lost. What is *lost* anyway?"

"Uh-oh. Here comes the philosophy."

"What's wrong with philosophy?"

"Well, it doesn't beat faith. Next thing, you'll be taking one of Greg Boyd's classes."

At Bethel, Professor Greg Boyd was dearly loved by a liberal niche of students because of his radical views regarding free will and determinism. Professor Boyd believed that free will and fate interact with each other dynamically. He believed that some things are planned by God and some things are left to choice. For many theologians at the Minnesota Baptist General Conference this was the equivalent of saying that God does not know the future, which means that God's knowledge is limited. Boyd was therefore thought to be a heretic, and during my time at Bethel there was a petition by members of the conservative administration and Baptist General Conference to remove Dr. Boyd from his duties as a Baptist Reverend and from his tenured position as a professor of theology at Bethel College.

For me Boyd's class was far more than an exercise in Christian rebellion. One day during class he brought a tape player and set it on top of his lectern. We listened to meditative music. He guided us into a state of meditation by the sound of his voice. He called the exercise contemplative prayer, but since I was simultaneously studying the only Eastern philosophy course Bethel offered, it seemed to me Dr. Boyd was conflating meditation and prayer either knowingly or secretively. I hoped secretively.

"This technique is as old as Jesus," Professor Boyd said. "It's just that we forget classic prayer was not simply petitionary. It wasn't just about asking for things you needed or praying for people who have it rough. It was also about spending time in the quiet and contemplating life. Being thankful for what you already have. Being reflective."

I laid my head on my desk in Professor Boyd's class and drifted into a deep state of relaxation. I saw myself sitting on the side of a mountain overlooking the Jordan River. There was a cool breeze. I felt things as if my vision were physical. The vision felt like a memory, and when my leg jerked awkwardly I startled at my desk, as if I had been gone for a long time. The way it feels when you walk into your bedroom again after being on vacation. After the meditation, somebody said, "That was like an acid trip."

"Not the same," Professor Boyd said. "I did acid once in college.

I even wrote a manifesto about my acid trip. But the next day the psychedelic manifesto made absolutely no sense to me. It was incoherent. Nothing I had written made any sense. I never did a psychedelic again. We don't need drugs to find meaning."

It was the only time I remember Greg Boyd sounding reactive, even angry. For a moment I wanted to try LSD in order to compare experiences. Something told me I might see something Professor Boyd was not able to see.

Each night after Professor Boyd's class I practiced contemplative prayer. I took meditation journeys into different worlds inside myself. During one meditation I saw pieces of the Statue of Liberty breaking apart and falling into the ocean. Big copper pieces quaking and breaking out like stress fractures of a towering eggshell, falling and shattering on the ocean as if the water were made of concrete. I wrote the strange vision in my journal after my meditation. The next morning, on September 11, the World Trade Center towers were destroyed by commercial jet planes. I was then twenty years old. I sat in front of the television set trying to share my vision with one of my roommates.

"That's very coincidental," he said.

"You don't think that's like prophetic or something?"

I showed my roommate my journal.

"Sure you aren't just making this up?"

"I saw it during my contemplative prayer last night," I said.

"Isn't that something Professor Boyd teaches? You know a lot of pastors consider him a heretic, right?"

When I told the visionary story to Stephanie, she agreed I should not be meditating and receiving visions or voices.

"It sounds evil," she said. "Have faith, but, you know, don't get weird or anything."

Soon after our conversation I broke up with Stephanie at a popular student diner down the street from Bethel.

"I smoke a lot of pot, and I've never told you because you would judge me. Shit, I go to worship services stoned on a regular basis, and I think it's breathtaking. And we don't really like any of the same things."

"God forgives us when we walk away from him," she said, teary eyed. "Don't forget that," she added, as if she were watching my soul start the slow walk toward hell.

Within a year Stephanie was engaged to a man on the soccer team. My only memory of her husband-to-be was of something he said one night when he smoked pot with me on the roof of the dormitory during the winter.

"Strip clubs are the best," he said. "Hot bitches and dancing. So nice to get out of here and do something fun from time to time."

I found it interesting that we were, in some ways, both disillusioned by the Christian lifestyle. Yet to him, marijuana and strip clubs were the same thing. Devious. Secret. Guy stuff. To me, they couldn't have been more different.

I turned twenty-one the summer before my last semester at Bethel and moved into an apartment off campus with a pot-smoking buddy who studied at the University of Minnesota. The nerve in my arm tightened up, and I could use my left hand again. The night before the first day of school, my mother arrived at my apartment door with puffy eyes and a tear-stained face. She wiped her nose with a Kleenex. She had made the fifteen-hour drive to St. Paul all the way from Michigan. Throughout college I only saw my family once or twice a year on average.

"Your father asked for a divorce and admitted the affair," she said as soon as I opened the door.

I looked at her with anger in my eyes. I put my hands on my hips.

"I told you," I said.

"He's depressed. He's so depressed, Adam. He wants out of the church. He wants out of our marriage. He wants out of his life. I'm worried he might hurt himself."

I remember my mom slept on my couch in the afternoon sunlight. I wished it were night, because sadness looks so sad during the middle of the day. Her legs curled up in the fetal position. She looked tired and alone. Not like a member of my family any longer. The sunlight long and hot on her blue jeans. Her socks looked nineteen. Her hair looked nineteen. And I was feeling not like her son but like her father, who had died of cancer shortly after she married *my father* at the young and sunny-afternoon age of nineteen.

CHAPTER 24

SINS OF THE FATHERS (III)

"Go put these wires into the truck."

The old man handed a sack full of copper wiring to his son. The teenage boy marched the heavy sack to the truck while his father disappeared back into the dark barn. Behind the truck was a trailer, and inside the trailer was a fat cow. It was snowing outside. The boy turned off his flashlight and rubbed his cold hands together. The ground was hard and slick. He looked up at the stars and moon. The air was thin and blue-white. Leaning against the trailer, the boy could see forever. The cow snorted steam out of its nose and stamped its foot up and down.

As my father waited for his father to finish the wiring job inside the barn, he contemplated his old man's motivation for stealing the copper wiring. His dad was a drunk and a chain-smoker and a son of a bitch, but the boy didn't figure him to be a crook. His old man worked him to the bone, sure, chopping wood all winter, tending the gardens, planting Christmas trees, dragging the two-track trails in the back forty, but he never once thought his dad was crooked. Driven, drunk, and mean as a bull, but not crooked.

As the boy and his father drove home along county road 46, the boy got up his courage to ask about the copper wiring, which he knew was the rightful property of the Michigan Mishcon Gas company. "What are you going to do with that copper wiring, Pop?"

"Keep your eye on the cow and make sure she doesn't slip. It's cold out there and she's probably scared shitless."

The boy looked through the back window of the truck at the cow in the trailer. Traveling fast down the highway in the dark, he could only see the cow's mournful face under the moonlight, muzzled and tied to the trailer bars. The cow was pulling its head back, struggling to break free from the grip of the rope.

"Pop, she's trying to get out of the rope!"

"She won't get nowhere. I tied that rope tight." Just as quickly as the boy's father had spoken, the truck's right tire slid off the edge of the road and onto the shoulder. The trailer followed with a loud crash. The cow made a high-pitched squealing noise that sounded human.

"What was that?"

"Goddammit!" said the boy's father.

Along the dark, wintry highway the truck slowed to a stop. The headlights pointed into the forest. The boy and his father hurried to see about the cow. They found the cow with its head jammed sideways between the trailer bars. The cow's neck was broken, and the rope wrapped around its eyes, pushing into the sockets. The cow was whimpering and crying.

"What are we going to do? It's got a broken neck." The boy stared at the cow with his mouth open. He could see the back of the cow's spine jutting out where it shouldn't have been. The cow's eyes darted back and forth.

The old man walked to the bed of the pickup truck and returned with a long-handled axe.

"You want to put it out of its misery?" The boy's lip quivered, and he looked at the cow and then at his father and then at the steel axe. The axe looked too big and heavy for him.

The boy's father walked to the cow's head and took six hard swings. Sparks flew when the axe blade rang off the trailer bars and into the cow's spine. There was a lot of blood, and the boy's father butchered the cow on the side of the road, taking a few small breaks to wash blood off his face with white snow. Right there under the moonlight. The boy watched. The cow whimpered the first two swings and was quiet after that.

The ride home felt empty, and the boy didn't talk.

"Don't ask questions unless you're ready for hard answers," his father said. "Crooks and thieves at the gas company. They're going to replace me with an engineer. He's got some fancy degree. Nobody respects hard work these days. I wouldn't be any good to you if I didn't work you hard. You could chop me up like that cow. You understand me? I would be no good to you."

He looked at his son and tried to smile. His son tried to hide his tears. The sight of which angered his father. "Damn it. I fought in the Korean War. Now, I know. There is no time for pain and crying about it. You've gotta be tough. Now bite your lip and tighten the slack."

CHAPTER 25

WALKING THE TALK

"Could I speak with Ethan?" I asked one of the apprentices, a tall white man in his fifties who wore gold wire-rimmed glasses.

"Why do you need to speak to him?"

"I'm going to leave camp early. But I'd like to speak with him about something personal before I leave. I have some questions I'd like to ask him."

"But you have two ceremonies left."

"I realize that," I said. "But I feel like it's time for me to go, and I'd really like to speak with Ethan about it."

The day that I left El Puma Negro was perhaps the most poignant moment in my ayahuasca journey to date. I still can't name who or what, exactly, led me down the dirt road from camp and onto a bus back into the city of Iquitos.

"He can talk to me in front of the group," Ethan had said of my request. He was speaking to a large crowd in the lodge about the illusion of duality, telling personal battle stories from countless ayahuasca ceremonies during his apprenticeship. Seeing him there with everybody gathered around him, for a moment I almost wanted to stay.

"I would like to speak in private, if we could."

"Talk to me right here," he said.

"Okay. Fine. I'd like to break my diet early and leave," I said.

"Did the plant spirits tell you it was okay to break your diet early?"

"Well, I want to speak to you about my decision in private."

"It's a simple question," he replied. "Are the medicine spirits telling you to leave?"

"All right," I retorted. "So, how do you know if the plant spirits are telling you it's okay to leave?"

"The only time I broke a diet, I had a one-hundred-and-four-degree fever."

"Right . . . Well, sure. I feel like the plant spirits are okay with my decision to leave now."

"Good. Then let's get moving. Domingo will give you a blessing, and you can go," he said.

"It doesn't have to be this minute," I said. "I want to speak with you a little bit."

"If you need to leave, then you should be on your way."

"All right," I said. My eyes filled with hot tears, and I made my way to my bungalow to gather my things.

Before I approached Ethan, I had sat in the meditation center for several hours, trying to make sense of it all. During ceremony the night before, a voice had spoken to me, a voice that seemed to transcend even the visions and the ayahuasca. Like someone deeply familiar, yet unidentifiable, the voice said, "You don't have to do this anymore. There is a big world out there for you to explore, and there are many beautiful shamans still to meet. It's time for you to leave now." As if the director of a play had suddenly appeared, saying, "Cut, cut, cut!" in a moment I knew even the ceremony happening around me was in some way just an act, that I was merely an actor playing my role.

It wasn't that the production of the event I was taking part in, or the drama of my life, was inauthentic, but rather that the unfolding of my entire existence, not just my visionary adventures in Peru, but my life since conception, had been observed and in some way directed or guided by something vast, unnamable, always present and kind. The lights offstage had come up and revealed a metaphysical audience of *one*, sitting right in front of me. At the same time, my body had instantly felt lighter and not so powerfully influenced or impressed by the effects of the ayahuasca.

In no way did I have negative feelings about the ceremony. Rather, it was as if I had found my regular self in the midst of the ritual, for the first time. The same me who might sit on my couch at home and read an interesting article on the Internet or drink a cup of hot tea in the morning after stretching out. There was something about me, no matter how transformational my experiences, that would always remain the same and had always been capable of making its own decisions. The voice that simultaneously appeared, saying, "You don't have to do this anymore," had made me feel as though I could trust the continuation of my life journey, and my exploration of ayahuasca medicine in particular, beyond the ceremonial mesa of El Puma Negro. In those moments, without any qualifications, I knew I would soon say good-bye. I knew, despite there being two more ceremonies left, I would be going home.

The only problem was that I loved El Puma Negro, and more than anything I loved Ethan and Domingo. I felt loyal to them, and I had received so much from my stays at camp. *I will need something logical and irrefutable to back up my decision to leave, won't I? I can't just leave without a reason and two ceremonies left in the retreat. I can't just say that some voice told me it's time to leave, can I? What will that look like? What will everyone think of me when they find out I'm leaving early?*

As I sat and pondered in the meditation center the next afternoon, I began to list arguments in my head as to why El Puma Negro had become, perhaps, questionable. Something tangible I could use to justify my decision to leave camp early. Something I could use to make my departure look more urgent or pressing—at least in my own head. After all, things *were* changing at El Puma Negro.

Ethan had become a celebrity shaman. That was my first line of reasoning. The price of attending a healing retreat had risen four times in three years. What had first cost me around eight hundred dollars was now nearly twenty-five hundred. In addition, a group of full-time apprentices had joined the staff at El Puma Negro, and the days were organized into miniature lecture groups and post-ceremony processing meetings, which the apprentices, all gringos, usually conducted.

At meals, Ethan, Domingo, and the apprentices ate at a separate table, and although Domingo was Ethan's teacher, he seldom spoke during ceremonies, while Ethan's speeches had gotten longer and more dogmatic. I sensed that something fundamental was changing at El Puma Negro since my first visit. However ancient ayahuasca medicine was, the traditional role of the ayahuasca shaman as doctor was shifting, at least in the person of Ethan Richter. Drinking ayahuasca was not just about getting healed by traditional *curanderos*; it was also becoming like a religion at El Puma Negro, a practice, something like regular meditation or yoga.

Also, there were so many people at the lodge, it was ridiculous. Nearly fifty in the mesa each night. And whereas Ethan had once been so personable with guests, now he hardly spoke to people except to give his own stylized shamanic sermons in front of the group. Whenever he walked into the lodge, people would turn their heads and stop talking. The entire mood and atmosphere would change, like a Hollywood movie star had entered the room. And Ethan had seemed to eat it up, always remaining stoic and rather irritated by any admirer who spoke to him personally, yet eager to expound upon his view of the universe if a group was gathered.

Because the camp was so big and there were so many people attending retreats, El Puma Negro had hired two nighttime security guards with rifles. Ever since the major magazine article about the lodge was published, the place had become like a resort, and all things considered, I couldn't help but feel like yet another spiritual leader had let his success get the best of him.

Thinking about things more, I also realized that perhaps El Puma Negro was not doing traditional shamanism any longer. Traditional ayahuasca shamanism, as I understood it, was about a doctor-patient relationship; if you were sick and needed help and you lived in the jungle, then you could go and see a *curandero*. But that's not exactly what was happening at El Puma Negro. Wires were being crossed. People were coming back to the lodge well after they'd been "healed" because Ethan was encouraging them to return and develop their own "medicine practice." It was as if Ethan wanted to be a doctor while simultaneously acting as the leader of a spiritual movement, like a charismatic ayahuasca preacher.

It felt to me like the historical difference between the Catholic Church and Protestantism. In the Catholic Church, the priest stood between the people and God, like a medium. But then Martin Luther had come along and said, "No way. Each person can and should contact the divine personally." And the role of the priest changed to the shepherdlike figure of the minister. Someone of the people and for the people.

Ethan, it seemed to me, was trying to play both cards. He wanted to be a medium for an experience with God, but then he also wanted to lead a spiritual movement in which everyone is equally divine, we're all shamans, and we should learn to heal ourselves and develop a personal relationship with the medicine. How could it work to play both roles at once?

When he stepped out of the way during ceremony, I felt abandoned. When he helped me, I felt resentful. Then he would preach to guests both ways: How he had gone through so much to become a doctor of the medicine. How the vocation of master shaman was a highly specialized spiritual calling—not just anyone could become a maestro; not just anyone could lead people through the visionary crucible and perform healings. Yet how important it was for us to have our own relationship with the medicine itself, to come back and drink diet plants (traditionally reserved for apprentices) and not to count on him or Domingo "babying" us during ceremonies, to master our own minds and further our "training." As if all the guests were both apprentices and patients at the exact same time. As if guests should know during the most intense psychological experiences of their lives when it was time to ask for help (as patient and clients of the master shamans conducting the ceremony) or when to fend for themselves (as future shamans in the making).

The confusion of Ethan's roles was never more apparent than within ceremonies themselves. As numbers in the mesa grew, he had developed an aggressive musical cadence that was punctuated by heavy staccatos, rhythmic beats of silence, pregnant pauses after every word, and a drill sergeant's "tough love" machismo. More and more, he would reprimand guests who asked for help with contradictory statements: "This is YOUR demon. YOU. Need to GET REAL. With YOURSELF. WE can't do the work FOR YOU. This is YOUR medicine practice. Ask YOURSELF for help."

Several breaths later he might sound off again to someone else, but address the entire group, saying, "If YOU don't listen to OUR ICAROS. And follow OUR guidance. YOU. WILL. GET. LOST. YOU are NOT shamans. You came HERE for HEALING and for HELP. Be REAL with yourselves."

While I liked the idea of ayahuasca being a personal practice, it seemed to me that the person of the shaman, or the way ceremonies were being led, should be changed in order to avoid confusion. I wondered if a collective ayahuasca leadership model existed or could be invented, or whether Ethan's role could be more clearly defined for people who practiced regularly, as opposed to those who came seeking healing for the first time. Some well-defined structure seemed necessary in order to establish boundaries between clients and shamans and between participants and "the medicine itself." I knew that I wasn't alone in thinking about it. I had noticed other people talking.

Everybody at camp, or at least the regulars, seemed to be gossiping about the changes at El Puma Negro, the distinct changes in Ethan's leadership style especially. Everyone had an opinion about everything, and every point of view had been "received in a vision." People were bickering and jockeying for power. Everybody wanted to be Ethan's next apprentice. Then I was starting to hear stories about Ethan himself. Earlier that week, a returning guest named David told me that Ethan had taken him on a motorcycle ride, just the two of them, and was talking to him about his apprentices, sharing personal secrets and business tactics with him. Some of the gossip David shared with me had been deeply disturbing. Ethan had spoken openly to David about staff indiscretions, shared private long-term business plans, and even boasted inappropriately about his sex life. David's gossip had made Ethan seem like a power-hungry chauvinist. And there was nothing in David's presentation that had led me to believe he was lying or fabricating a story about Ethan for attention. I knew David to be a reliable and intelligent guy. As a result, my first reaction was not disbelief but shock. Ethan had saved my life at least a dozen times in the mesa. How could he tell someone like David, a guest (who obviously couldn't keep his mouth shut), his secrets? To me, it wasn't just disappointing to have Ethan's and Domingo's characters called into question, it was like betrayal. I felt betrayed by Ethan for having shared such sensitive information with a guest. And then betrayed by David for brushing off my reaction to the gossip.

"That's heavy stuff," I said.

"Shamans are just human, man," David said.

"Yeah, but do you have any idea what it does to a religious community when the leader is exposed for acting hypocritically? It can be devastating."

"Only because people put shamans up on pedestals."

"I don't buy that line of reasoning," I said. "Sure, people put a lot of expectations onto religious leaders. Making a mistake and then speaking to the community about it is one thing. I think people have a lot of forgiveness for that. But privately sharing indiscretions with certain church members, never the community as a whole, that's something else. I don't think it's right."

"Why should he need the forgiveness of the entire group? Or anybody in particular? It's between him and God, man."

"So why did he share it with you? To me, the medicine experience is filtered through the person of the shaman in these ceremonies. More than anybody else in the mesa, those guys need to be clean and open about what they are dealing with. That's the responsibility of their position, I think."

"It's like you expect Ethan to be Jesus Christ himself. You're putting things onto him."

"No way," I said. "He's the one whose talking back and forth about how hard it is to become a shaman, how much responsibility it entails, yet how we are all shamans. And anyway, it doesn't even sound like he was telling you these things from a place of remorse. Bragging about his sexual conquests? That's just juvenile."

"It's not like he's married yet! Maybe you're just upset because your father was a preacher, and he was unfaithful to your mom."

"That's my point exactly," I said. "You don't go sharing personal secrets like that when someone like me is one of your guests at camp. I think it's irresponsible. It muddies the water."

"Well, when you get to know Ethan personally like I have, after you drink in more ceremonies, and heal up from all this stuff with your dad, you'll see everything clearly. Crystal clear and no muddiness. He's a lot cooler than you know just yet."

I felt naive to think I had found a little slice of perfection, tucked away in the Amazon. And I wondered what people back home would think of me if a scandal at El Puma Negro were to ever break the news. I was trekking across the planet on expensive, oil-hungry airplanes. Probably destroying the rain forest at the same rate I was learning about it. And what if I had been nothing more than a tourist the whole time? Just some punk white kid whose parents didn't show him enough love and who picked up some bad habits and had to come to the jungle to puke and moan. Only to be let down by yet another hypocritical preacher. . . .

For several hours my internal dialogue tried to organize and compartmentalize each and every reason I had for leaving. The hard part was that it honestly was not about any of my best reasons for leaving. In some ways each and every bit of my logic was correct, yet something didn't feel right. When I imagined myself confronting Ethan to accuse him or El Puma Negro of any particular offenses, I felt hypocritical. I couldn't end my relationship with Ethan on a self-righteous or sour note. Not when considering the lessons I had learned in my time at El Puma Negro.

Whatever I had to say, and regardless of his faults, Ethan had followed a calling all the way to the jungle, from his life as a troubled twentysomething in the United States. He had lived in the middle of the rain forest. Swum and bathed with natives. Harvested his own food. Built his own home with his own hands, out of the jungle itself. Drunk in hundreds of ceremonies and trained in one of the most intense psychological settings in the world—the visionary space of ayahuasca. His mission was to build a place for Westerners to come and learn about a different culture and an incredible tradition. Not just as a source of revenue but in order to heal people. In order to teach people. There would always be goodness in that. And if I couldn't see good in that, then I hadn't learned anything about my cynicism yet. Ethan and Domingo had helped me through the most intense transformational moments of my life to that point.

Also, I could never forget how I showed up at El Puma Negro with so little trust in myself or other people. How everything had changed, and I had learned to trust life so fully. I could never forget when Domingo called the thunder and the entire mesa shook with white light. Or the time Ethan held my hand for two straight hours and sang me songs when I didn't even know my own name. How toward the end he had told me, "Forgive your father. We're all doing the best we can. See the best in everyone." How I had cried so hard, my entire body convulsed for thirty minutes straight. How good my dad's voice sounded on the telephone in the airport on the way home. How even though he still wasn't perfect, I actually loved him again. So deeply, I could literally feel sensations in my bones every time we spoke for the next six months. And that was it. Those things had happened at El Puma Negro. Throughout my time there, I had learned so much.

So my departure wasn't about needing a reason to discard or discredit my time at El Puma Negro in order to leave. As a matter of fact, I had been doing that for way too long. Discrediting my father and joining the Baptist church. Discrediting my family and going to Bethel. Competing with my father and becoming a youth pastor. Leaving Chicago because it was such a "heavy, rotten" place. What was I going to do next? Go out and try to become a shaman on my own? Start my own lodge? Write a treatise about El Puma Negro and nail it to the mesa door? Walk away from camp like it was the burning cities of Sodom and Gomorrah? I might have been right about what was going on with Ethan and Domingo, and camp in general, but if I was right, then I needed to let God or spirit or the medicine sort it out. In fifteen years, I wanted to look back at my life and have burnt as few bridges as possible. Wasn't it the medicine itself, or God, or something trustworthy that had led me to El Puma Negro, anyway? And wasn't it God who had spoken to me in ceremony the night before and told me it was time to leave? Isn't there a higher voice guiding all of us?

So when Ethan refused to talk with me in private when I decided to go, when he made me speak to him, standing in front of the group, my feelings were deeply hurt. My only intention had been to share my inner process, get clarity about the gossip circulating, tell him about the voice I had heard saying it was time to go, and to say thank-you before leaving.

Maybe I was setting him up to be another father figure who could disappoint me, so he tested my resolve. Maybe he wanted me to come to my own conclusions, so he tested me in front of the group. Or maybe his ego was out of control, and he had become a celebrity shaman. Regardless, I had made the decision to leave and was sticking to it.

When I reached the end of the dirt road leading from the camp at El Puma Negro, David (the guest who had taken the motorcycle ride with Ethan) was already sitting on the pavement, camped on top of his duffle bag, with a dejected look on his face.

"You're leaving, too?" I asked.

"Ethan asked me to take a little break from El Puma Negro to get some perspective."

"I'm sorry to hear that. You okay?"

"I'm totally fine with it. I'm thinking of going to India. If it's not my time to apprentice, then it's not my time. I never should have shared that stuff with you. I ought to have known you weren't ready to hear it."

"Yeah," I said. "Maybe I wasn't."

"I'll be back, though." He cut me off. "I'll prove myself again. The spirits obviously have some lessons for me to learn. I'll prove to them that I'm not attached to earning the title of master shaman."

On the bus ride back to Iquitos, breezing down the Nauta highway and sitting next to a dead-quiet David, who had no gossip left to report and was ignoring me as if it were his duty, I noticed for the first time in all of my bus rides down that road the colorful signs of the neighboring ayahuasca lodges. There were so many of them: the Holy Condor, the Yellow Anaconda, Espíritu de los Elementos. Seeing them, I felt a mixture of emotions. I felt sad picturing myself at another lodge with different shamans. Ashamed, as if I had been cast out. And then disappointed by Ethan and El Puma Negro all over again. As the bus finally descended a cobblestone hill into the city of Iquitos and hundreds of people came into sight, standing next to fruit carts and palm trees, the sky above looking like it would rain, I reminded myself that the decision had been my own. I had trusted the voice inside me. And if it was true, and ayahuasca shamanism was becoming a global spiritual movement, then there was a whole world out there to explore.

CHAPTER 26

SON OF A PREACHER MAN

"Is that pot I smell?" my father asked. We had been packing boxes all evening in my apartment when he smelled my roommate smoking grass from his bedroom. College was over.

"Yes, sir," my roommate answered.

"You got any extra for an old man?"

"Yes, sir!"

"Are you serious?" I asked.

"Do you have a problem with it?"

"No way," I said. I laughed in disbelief. "Enjoy yourself."

The next morning when my dad asked me if I wanted to roll a joint before we hit the road, I said, "Absolutely."

It was funny to see my father roll a joint. His fingers suddenly nimble and fast. I watched his movements with a plastic lighter, his lips and tongue, sharp fingers and quick eyeballed measurements against the thin rolling paper; the muscle memory was still there, as if it hadn't been more than a day or two since he'd been a college student playing his guitar and buying pot in parking lots.

"Does Mom know you're smoking?"

"She doesn't know anything. She would leave me, man. I've already messed everything up. I just want to relax. I feel down all the time. I'm trying here, okay, man. I really am."

"Don't feel bad, man," I said. I passed my father the joint. We sat in the front seat of the cold moving truck.

"Yeah, man," my dad finally said. I realized it was the third or fourth time we had said the word "man" to each other within a minute. The word had presented itself like a riddle for the two of us to sit with, awkwardly, as we started to forget the joint was burning.

Who was this person sitting next to me? It occurred to me there were more things unknown between us than there were unsaid. Like, *Why aren't you guys divorcing each other?*

We had never sat down as a family to talk about it. We had never had a family vacation to regroup. We never did family counseling, either. Instead, my father called me on the telephone one night, sweeping things under the carpet with an embarrassed apology.

"I'm sorry," he said. "You'll understand someday."

I thought to myself, *I will never understand because I'm never going to cheat on my wife, asshole.* But instead I said, "We all make mistakes."

"You can be angry at me," my dad said.

"I've known about your secret affair for a long time, and I've had a while to talk to God about it," I replied, pretending I had developed an advanced moral conscience. I was being an *adult* about it.

"I'd like to move forward and try again," he said.

"Whatever you need to do. It's really between you and God. We can only imitate his love by forgiving each other," I answered.

Anger felt uncomfortable to me. I knew that anger was an inappropriate way to communicate with my father, but at the core I felt nothing *but* angry. My spiritually "centered" responses were a façade used to circumvent my rage.

It wasn't that I needed to hear some particular words or even an apology; it was that I needed to know things I couldn't understand on principle, needed face-time for my ears to open wide enough to hear why nobody was talking. The word "forgiveness" and all of the scriptures I'd ever been taught were no substitute for the intimacy I craved. Since I did not know how to ask for the attention I needed without anger and conflict, I created a false empathy and pointed at God as though he'd given it to me, as though he'd blessed me with more adult qualities than my parents', as if Jesus himself had raised me into a "man of God" during my time at Bethel.

The funny thing was that my father's ministry, over the years, had become plagued by the same malaise. Once church work had become no different than what my grandfather always called the rat race, void of intimacy and authentic friendships, and unable to disclose his own doubts, his anger, or his need for respite, my father's mental health started to collapse under the pressure of a clergyman's duties.

After I graduated from Bethel my dad helped me move from Minneapolis to Chicago to start my first job as the youth minister of a large Methodist church. Even now I'm not sure why I did it. By that time I had lost interest in fundamentalist Christianity, broken up with my Baptist girlfriend, and was embarrassed to discover that my evangelical Pentecostal, etc., etc., had been, at least in part, my version of teenage rebellion. I still can't be sure if I was being competitive with my dad or if I was trying to find common ground, a way to forgive him; maybe all of these at the same time. I know that my father's words had been mortared into whatever cracks of vulnerability I had accidentally exposed to him when he ever so briefly apologized: *You'll understand someday.*

Together, we drove a pickup truck (borrowed from my grandfather) filled with possessions enough to fill my first small studio apartment: a rusty twin bed from Goodwill, a beat-up old couch, some half-burnt candles, a guitar, my stereo, and my clothing. Symbolically, that morning on the drive to Chicago, the *Columbia* space shuttle disintegrated over Texas on its way back into the earth's atmosphere. Although my father and I had taken a step in the right direction (as unorthodox as it might have been for a preacher and his son to smoke a peace pipe filled with cannabis), I feared the shuttle explosion was a bad omen. I was afraid reentry into an atmosphere of love would prove impossible. My father was moving me, but I couldn't feel him guiding me, and I wasn't sure what life was supposed to look like in the adult world outside Bethel.

"Life is like a big, difficult, and confusing maze," I said from the pulpit. I spoke a small sermon for a large group of Methodist students gathered in the sanctuary for a Friday night slumber party. I was the youth pastor of a large suburban church, and I was twenty-two years old.

"In order to know God, we have to know difficulty. It has to be difficult and confusing," I said. It was dark in the sanctuary. Holding on to their sleeping bags and pillows, fidgeting and nervous, the students looked shocked in their pews.

Before the slumber party I had spent weeks collecting cardboard boxes from warehouses, grocery stores, and back-alley dumpsters. I placed announcements in the church bulletin and collected nearly seven hundred boxes, of all shapes and sizes. The idea for the maze had crossed my mind one evening after smoking several joints and drinking a pint of whiskey by myself. I thought, *Life must be a maze by nature, and we all have to make our way out. That's just reality. Reality is suffering.* Poof! My object lesson presented itself. *You should build a maze out of hundreds of cardboard boxes and make the kids crawl through it in the church basement. You could talk about how knowing God is like trying to find your way out of a maze. What better way to wake kids up to the difficult truth!*

I stayed in my church office late at night and drafted the outline of the maze, being careful to add secret sliding doors and mirrors and dark music into the maze blueprints, and taking small pot breaks as I schemed, escaping to the day-care playground behind the church.

When the day arrived, I spent twelve hours building the maze with a team of volunteer workers. After fifty rolls of duct tape, my existential object lesson was complete. The entrance to the tunneled maze started at the top of a long stairwell behind the church altar. The staircase was covered in a box tunnel slide and crashed into a pit in the basement that led into the fellowship hall. As each one of the children slid down the box slide, a wireless microphone cleverly planted inside the chute captured the cries of each student, screaming and fading voices over the church PA system into the black hole of the basement.

"Life isn't easy. It's just not," I had said from the pulpit as the kids entered the maze one by one. I felt a certain inspiration. "God is a mystery. He's full of secrets we can only discover by suffering. It's what builds our spiritual character."

"I don't want to go in the maze," one of the younger students said with a terrified look on her face.

"You're already in it!" I said. "It's called life. So you might as well enjoy it and find your way out!"

"This is totally awesome," said one of the older boys.

The music was eerie and trancelike, the kind of thing you would hear at a dingy club in downtown Chicago, not a church sleepover in the suburbs. A handful of strobe lights flickered in key locations. I heard the sounds of my older students giggling and enjoying themselves. Many of the younger children were afraid. The adult volunteers cut a hole in the side of one box to release several of the young ones who were claustrophobic. One of the little girls started complaining: "Oh God, let me out of here. I'm stuck. I can't see anything."

"That's right," I said. "We're all stuck!"

Others joked, "Is that you? Where are we? This is so cool. Is that your hand or mine?" For hours the students played in the maze, and everything was going according to my plan until one of my adult volunteers approached me.

"Adam," he said. "I caught the high school boys. I think they were smoking *marijuana* on the playground outside." He whispered the word "marijuana" to me as if it were the secret ingredient to a treasured family recipe. "I have them waiting in your office to speak with you. Do you want me to call the police?"

An hour before the children arrived, I had smoked an entire joint myself behind the church, and there was no way I was going to pass the pot smoker's litmus test. Like all stoners know: When you're high you feel the other members of your society by proxy. All stoners can spot another stoner trying to pass himself off as sober. One giggle can flip the script.

"No, no, I'll take care of it," I said. "No police. I've got this under control."

I was going into my office, full of my stoner church students, high as a kite, and I was going to try convincing them that it was inappropriate to be stoned, especially because we were at church.

Each one of the boys reeked of dank weed and fruity, ripe cologne. One of the boys stashed a bottle of eye drops as soon as I entered the office. Another boy put the hood of his sweatshirt over his face. The others looked at their feet.

"Look," I said, trying not to make eye contact or giggle. "He wants me to call the police or your parents and send you home. I can't let you get away with it. They won't understand if I let you off the hook. Why were you smoking pot, anyway? How stupid can you be to do that at church?"

One of my students spoke up. "Dude, your maze is awesome. We just wanted to get high before we went through it again. Tell me you don't think it would be cool to get stoned and trip out inside of that thing!"

"No, I don't think it would be *cool*," I lied. "Marijuana can lead to a lot of . . . umm . . . messed up stuff."

"Like what?"

"Well," I stammered. "It's a gateway drug," I said. "You never know what kind of funny things you can get into when you smoke grass."

The words felt funny coming out of my mouth, like a foreign authority had entered my body, or like I was casting a hex upon myself.

"*Grass?*" one of the boys asked sarcastically. They all started giggling.

"Listen. Tell him you were smoking clove cigarettes and that I took them from you. Say that you're sorry, and ask him to forgive you, okay?"

After the labyrinth it was obvious to me I had no idea what I was doing. Repeating similarly ironic failures in my duties as a youth pastor and dealing with parental complaints on a regular basis, I resigned from my position within a year and decided to return to graduate school. I knew I shared a religious destiny with my father. Truth be told, he had come up with the maze idea in the first place. I lied to everyone about it being my idea. When I was a little boy he had built a maze in the church basement for the older kids and then finally built one for me in the basement of the parsonage after I begged him long enough. Except there was no explicit message about being lost in the darkness or finding God. As a kid, it was just a fun game to play on a Friday night while locked inside the church.

During the eight-month period between my resignation from my job as a youth pastor and the beginning of graduate school, I entered into a self-destructive vortex. During the spring I sat on my porch near the city el-train tracks smoking cigarette after cigarette. I smoked a pack of American Spirits a day, and my weed bill was steady at two hundred dollars a week. Credit card bills lay scattered across my kitchen table: six, seven, eight thousand dollars' worth of cash advances from credit lines at rising interest rates, unfixed variables, numbers and phrases I didn't understand. Constant telephone calls from credit collectors. I lived on credit cards, but I told my family I saved money. I told my worried mother, "I'm fine, really. Everything is fine."

Then it was an online-dating habit gone bad. At hotornot.com I would meet impressionable women through pictures and testimonials and impress them inside Internet chat rooms until we could meet in person. I would promise things: relationships, a future, a life together, and I would read poetry and play music and whisper little white lies (painful stories twisted to impress). *So I took off to study Paul's footsteps around the Mediterranean by myself. I met this beautiful Greek girl in the cave of the Apocalypse. Unrequited love. Yeah. I just wanted to go see the world. Go find myself.* Then we would drink alcohol and get naked in furious exchanges next to open windows and cheap Christmas lights strung up in my studio apartment. Something called "making love."

But by the next day, without fail, I found a way to make sure I never had to speak to any of the girls again. The occasional girl left one last message to say her period was late or that I was an asshole. I worried myself sick into bottles of whiskey, often ignoring telephone calls, trying to avoid conflict or bad news.

Within six months I had slept with approximately sixty different women. It's embarrassing to know that I lost track, and even more embarrassing to know that I was averaging one to two different sexual encounters a week in the city through online-dating websites.

When I came down with the clap three times over the summer, I started drinking alcohol every night to ease the pain of my stinging genitals. I drank three to four shots of hard liquor, 151 proof, and then several bottles of beer every night before either entertaining a new woman from the Internet or settling into a blur of frustrated blogging. Having sex without protection and without telling my partners I was recently off antibiotic treatment had an extremely negative effect: often after ejaculating I felt immense amounts of unexplainable physical pain, followed by emotional release: crying, shaking, and even vomiting.

One night, at a woman's apartment in Wrigleyville, my top finally blew. She was an elementary school teacher I seduced into sex after an all-day trip to the Shed Aquarium. By promising her a serious relationship, I got her to sleep with me.

"Are you crying in there?"

"I'm fine," I said between sobs. I sat in her bathroom. The head of my penis pulsed with fire and pain. I heard voices chattering, and my body felt too sensitive, like the littlest things were hot irons pressing into my nervous system.

"No. Tell me what's wrong. You just bolted out of bed right after you came."

"I said I'm fine. I just can't do this anymore. This has to stop."

"Can't do what? Wait? What has to stop? What are you saying?"

"I'm fucked up. I'm sorry," I said. "It's not you. I'm just not ready for relationships and sex. I can't have sex anymore. All this sex is killing me."

"Well this isn't a confessional box, so get the fuck out of my apartment, you little shit. I knew you were full of it. You little pussy."

She pounded and kicked on the bathroom door until I came out of the bathroom and gathered my belongings as she pounded my body and face with her fists, blocking the door, in tears, screaming and swinging her fingers and nails like stray bullets. I shoved her out of the way and across the room. She stumbled backward and fell onto her back, painting falling off the wall, and coffee table tipping over onto its side with a loud thud, and I ran down three flights of stairs to the rushing city streets. I ran blocks and blocks looking for a taxi.

When I returned to my apartment I drank myself to sleep, lying naked in my shower, waking only when the water turned so cold it forced me into chills and vomiting, and I fumbled to turn the faucet. I woke in the morning covered only by a towel, lying in a puddle of stomach acid on the tiles of my bathroom floor.

In cycles I tried to stop seducing women by looking at pornography and masturbating instead. I smoked cigarettes, drank alcohol, smoked pot, and watched sex videos when I felt tempted to find single women on websites. A sick pattern ensued. After each time I ejaculated I was consumed by voices and the feeling of a physical dissociation from my body. The voices would sometimes tell me to do things: *fuck yourself, throw yourself off the balcony, walk into traffic, drink until you die.* I would soak under hot water until I felt stable. I would press my face against the needles of my shower mat for hours at a time, asking God to make the voices go away. Then I would stay up late, reading about schizophrenia until I felt sure that wasn't happening to me. Not *that.* I would take Tylenol PM and chase it with whiskey to knock myself out.

CHAPTER 27

SELF-CENTERED

Four small candles quivered in the night. Each candle sat on the edge of a fabric altar laid in the center of the mesa. On top of the altar sat rocks and gemstones of all different colors. Little hand-carved statues made of wood. Animals. Mythological creatures. Gods and goddesses.

It was my first ceremony in the United States and my first with a new shaman since leaving El Puma Negro. Very quickly, by making only a few mouse clicks on the Internet, I had discovered underground spiritual communities where people were flying in shamans from South America to do regular ceremonies at yoga studios and retreat centers all over the country. Skeptical again that I wouldn't be participating in the "real" ayahuasca experience, I avoided the homeland ceremonies for two years. But as my windows for traveling to South America for weeks at a time were dwindling, and my desire to continue healing with ayahuasca increased, I finally decided to try a local ceremony with a visiting shaman I knew to be a reputable *curandero* from Peru.

An hour into the ceremony, which was held at a yoga studio, I could still taste the molten ayahuasca on my tongue, and my body felt drunk. I wanted to be sick but did not know why. Something was trying to purge its way out.

"I have a question," I said. Carlos stopped pounding his water drum. A wealthier, urban ayahuasca shaman, Carlos had spent a number of years traveling the world and had also trained extensively with Navaho medicine men, in addition to his primary ayahuasca training in the jungle.

"I want to purge, but I don't know why. I'm not having any visions. It just feels like I'm sick. Could you sing an *icaro* and make me vomit?"

"Why don't you ask the candles to show you," he said. He spoke semifluent English, impressive for a visiting South American shaman. "You have to learn to ask the elements. The air. The fire. The waters. The earth. *Icaros* are only one medicine tool we can use to work with ayahuasca. Why don't you ask the fire for advice instead of thinking with your head?"

An elder woman from India who was sitting next to me smiled warmly, urging me to look into the fire. I had been sitting next to her all night and had never once made eye contact with her. When I looked into her eyes I felt safe. She was sitting on her knees with her hands in her lap, folded in prayer.

I crawled on my hands and knees toward the altar like a little boy.

When I got to the altar, I sat down in front of one of the candles and thought to myself, *Here goes nothing*. I reached my hand out to grab one of the four candles and hold it.

"No," Carlos said. "Not like that. The fire is alive. Would you go up to a stranger in the market and act like she wasn't there and then say, 'Hey, you, why don't you tell me something I need to know?'"

"No," I said. "I wouldn't. I get it, okay." As a shaman, Carlos was very different from Ethan and Domingo, much more like the wisecracking Yoda from *Star Wars*, and I struggled to take him seriously. I was not enjoying sitting on a yoga mat. I missed the jungle sounds, and I was not convinced ayahuasca shamanism could become a syncretic discipline. Let the Navahos be Navaho and let ayahuasca shamanism be led by the singing of *icaros*.

"No, you don't *get it*." Carlos snapped back at me, as if he had read each one of my thoughts. "You think you're better than the fire. You don't respect the fire. You have big spiritual ideas in your head, but they're all about *you*. It's very rude. You need to show respect if you want real friends and community. You came from the Christian tradition, didn't you?"

"Yes," I said. I wondered how Carlos knew.

"It's written very deeply on your heart. It's good. Jesus was a good healer. You want life eternal, huh? Then you have to see everything alive. The same. Treat others the same as yourself. Value them as much as yourself. Value other practices. Learn about them. Be creative. Learn to value what is outside yourself and put your money where your mouth is."

Defeated but not convinced, I said, "So what do I do right now?"

"Approach the candle with respect and care. Be gentle. Ask permission nicely to pray with the candle. Then meditate and ask for an answer."

I took a deep breath and focused on the candle for several moments. I watched it dance and sway. I watched it burn steadily, and I began to see it clearly. The candle wasn't simply moving. It was eating oxygen in its own dance and poetry. I brought my face slowly to the candle and looked closely into its light. When my face was just an inch from the flame, I asked the flame my question: "Would you please help me? Why do I feel so sick right now? If I'm a divine being, then why should I have to struggle all the time?"

"*Ahhh,*" Carlos said. "Now you are listening. What do you hear?"

Staring at the candle I began to drift out of my body. Sitting squarely with the candle in my palm, a vision drifted out the center of my forehead and swirled into the mesa. I found myself floating on my back down a deep, blue river underneath innumerable stars. A warm breeze moved over the surface of the waters, and I could see thousands of small, red-pink lights on the top of the water, moving and bobbing with the downstream current. I could hear the slow beat of a drum, making the sky look like liquid. Everything trembled.

"What is this?" I asked.

Then I came close to one of the lights on top of the water and realized that it was a tiny human fetus cocooned in a small gelatin sack, pulsing with a bright pink light as it floated down the river. The baby looked almost alien with pitch black eyes, curled into the fetal position, a bag of crimson light and plasmatic blood, streaming this way and that through its miniscule veins and arteries. The drum kept beating in the sky.

Looking at fibers so complex and tightly woven but so fragile, I saw into the blueprints of human life: The amniotic ocean. The pain of separation. A drumbeat. The stranglehold of the birth canal. The trauma of new life. The blank self. A drumbeat. The oceanic mind. The development of self, the growing of limbs, the learning of lessons, and beating drums for rites of passage. Then the marriage of heaven and hell: sexuality, adulthood, family, new children, cascading into the silence of old age. A drumbeat. And then death, withering from the macrocosm of big black eyes and then once more into the tiniest pink pulse of life, floating down the river. Thumping little beats in the canyons of space.

The water shallowed, and I stood in the gravel and stone bed of the river. The water reached my chest. I watched the pink lights as they sailed mightily downstream to whatever ocean awaited them, a parade of unborn babies floating without purpose toward a bright pink light on the watery horizon.

"This must be heaven," I thought. "This is where we go when we die."

Then I heard a voice in the sky singing a soothing mantra over and over again, and I recognized the voice as that of the Indian woman sitting next to me in the ceremony. Carlos had asked her to sing for me in the mesa. In the sky I saw her face smiling in the stars, and I watched as hundreds of the little red lights began to whisk off the surface of the water.

"Where are you going?" I began to splash and struggle. I could feel my fingers digging into the floorboards. I wanted to stay there forever. I didn't want the babies to leave. A place without decisions. A place that moves itself and beats on and on and on. That place where I'm a child again. That place where I am loved. That place where I am safe. Red lights. Pink lights. Heartbeat. Stars. Supernova. Nobody should have to leave.

"I knew she had an abortion," I said, back in the mesa. I held the candle in my open hand. "When I lived in Chicago. I knew it. I knew it was happening the whole time, and I ignored her. I was a bad father. I abandoned my child. I was afraid to take responsibility." I set the candle back on the altar, sensing the onset of a purge.

I held my stomach and choked out apologies and long strands of pink beads from my stomach. Each bead was the feeling that I was a murderer, that I had murdered an innocent child. Drumbeats, like little bolts of sadness and guilt, swept through my body like fiery tremors. I shook in the current of purging noises and vomit, possessed by the memory of an ignored abortion. My pores opened, and I began to sweat profusely, pink lights leaving my skin as my body danced inside like the little candle.

The Indian woman spoke to me. "In India we sing a song that helps spirits on their way. Sometimes we don't let spirits go when they die. We think we're making them safe by keeping them with us, but really we're keeping them for ourselves. So we sing them on their way. We pray to the fire to burn off our attachments to the dead soul, otherwise we grieve too long and become like hardened wax."

"You see," Carlos said to me. "There are many things for you to learn from. The fire. Songs from India. Many things for you to learn. And you don't have to be worried about whether or not you are a killer. Now you should forgive yourself and forgive other people. You're not the only one in this reality. Being self-centered is not the same as knowing yourself."

CHAPTER 28

THE SHAMANIC FINE PRINT

People commonly misunderstand the visionary to be someone who wants to do away with boundaries all together. But this is not true. While growing we must remember that what appears "expansive" or "open-minded" may not be healthy. This was a problem during our first cultural vision quest in the United States, which happened during the 1960s.

The 1960s were a mind-opening rite of passage. Millions of people took mind-expanding drugs that brought bigger visions of self and society. The environmental movement was born. Feminism gained more momentum than ever before. Civil rights won major victories. People demanded an end to the Vietnam War. Rock 'n' roll was the driving force of personal expression, and global networking devices like the personal computer began their rise toward the development of the World Wide Web. One could safely say the 1960s were an elevation of consciousness.

However, the psychedelic 1960s are now sometimes mocked as a "failed experiment," or as "youthful idealism." There was violent protest. There was self-righteous condemnation of culture and religion by people taking LSD. Guitars were burned onstage. Protests became violent. People recklessly mixed drugs and took psychedelic "trips" without shamanic tradition or guidance. Many died of overdose and inexperience. Political leaders were assassinated, and hypocrites were "outed" in every single national community. As a result of the mixed messages, the cultural era is often reduced to its material nostalgia: a Woodstock DVD, a tie-dyed T-shirt, a family visit to the Rock 'n' Roll Hall of Fame, the symbol of a protesting fist in the air, or a black light and a Beatles poster.

People now pejoratively call others hippies, when they want to describe someone who is "inconsistent," "lazy," "naive," "idealistic," and "self-destructive." The problem with the 1960s is that self-destruction was associated with mind expansion. In other words, while some oppressive boundaries were broken, other healthy boundaries were not kept holy. Many former hippies now associate their old psychedelic experiences with the hedonistic behaviors that accompanied them. The vision quest is often scrutinized because of its association with the drug culture of the unruly '60s and '70s.

I generally empathize with older generations that assume the vision quest is about escapism. If we look closely at the United States' experience with visionary shamanic medicine over the past few centuries, it is easy to see how this perception originated.

Our country was founded by people seeking freedom. At the core of this quest was a mixed bag of emotions and intentions. Many of the first immigrants to the United States were thieves, murderers, and pagans in their homelands of Europe. There is something at the heart of our cultural heritage steeped in rebellion. A problem arises when we try to see our nation's collective psychic history as one of pure pedigree.

While our founding revolution led to the establishment of a democracy, we also slaughtered the indigenous people and stole land instead of asking permission to join the already established societies. This basic moral history lesson proves that our American rebellion and liberation was mixed with anger as well as idealism. After all, we struggled to give women the right to vote and create equality among the skin colors for the first 150 years of our nation's existence. It's clear to see that we have been far from perfect.

On the other hand it would be a mistake to suggest the indigenous people living here were without tribal warfare, witchcraft, and personal troubles. The story of every native tribe on earth since the dawn of time includes great conflicts and resolutions. The problems in any culture come when the culture forgets its past. A great nation becomes dangerous when it forgets the moments that shaped its integrity and instead becomes arrogant about its success. A poor winner is not the same thing as a visionary.

The same can be said about any vision quest. If we mistake expansion for hedonism, then we will not learn anything and mind expansion will not be understood. Our visions will not be clearly felt. Transformation can be painful, but it doesn't have to be violent. Every vision we have as human beings is still happening from our bodies here on earth. It is important that we take good care of ourselves and other people, knowing how to stay safe and respectful along the way.

Even though ayahuasca ceremonies dissolve boundaries they also impart a deep sense of responsibility and discipline. Here are five important insights I've had since drinking ayahuasca.

1. **I stopped using drugs.** Ayahuasca medicine ceremonies are not recreational. They are sacred, guided, purposeful, and transformational rituals. It might seem strange, but every single ayahuasca ceremony shows me the joy of a sober life. As each ceremony progresses I learn to focus my mind and avoid being taken over by visions. The few times I've drunk alcohol since working with ayahuasca, for example, have been unenjoyable. The use of recreational drugs is not healthy for me. While I am thankful for every one of my past experiences and am always amazed at the way in which marijuana and psychedelics brought me to ayahuasca in the first place, since I drank ayahuasca my life has been sober.

2. **I am generally not a proponent of psychedelics for "fun."** While the psychedelic experience is meaningful, I also think it can be dangerous. I have met too many people who have suffered long-term mental health problems because of using substances like LSD compulsively and without guidance. I generally tell people that if they are seeking a mind-expanding vision quest it is best to seek a tradition with guidance and context. Not every psychedelic experience will end badly, but many can and often do. While bad psychedelic trips have often traumatized me and even harmed my nervous system, I have

never once experienced anything but healing with the guidance of shamans and ayahuasca ceremonies. The truth is that people do not need a psychedelic to learn, grow, or heal. Generally speaking, psychedelics without guidance and context are grab bag experiences. I do not recommend them. I also think that when used hedonistically, psychedelics give visionaries a murky reputation.

3. **I do not believe in free love.** I mean that I do not believe in equating boundary expansion and the visionary experience with orgies, sex parties, and seduction or with adultery, pornography, and lust. Most of the time those experiences are about an attempt to objectify the human mind, the human body, and reality itself. Whatever forms of sexuality a person chooses there is no excuse for betrayal, lies, deception, jealousy, violence, abuse, or neglect. That is not free love. Free love means respect, honesty, authenticity, intimacy, gratitude, joy, humor, and humility.

4. **I do not accept everything.** Many people suggest that to believe in the infinite, nonjudgmental, and universal God means accepting the bad things, like brutality and violence. Acceptance is the nature of reality. Everything is always accepted by God whether we want to accept it or not. Since that is the truth, I do not see the point in violence and human darkness. Violence is born when people do not understand the fact that reality is accepting. Violence is an attempt to fight against acceptance itself, and it never succeeds. Therefore I do not accept violence insofar as I see it as unnecessary. There is a better way.

5. **I still believe in evangelism.** We don't have to try to be anything. We are always ourselves. We are always authentic. We are always where we are supposed to be. We are always meaningful. I believe these things because I have experienced them. I believe that there is nothing at stake. The purpose of evangelism then is to create heaven on earth. When we stop pretending to be somebody else and act authentically, from our hearts, it is the "good news," the real Gospel, which every single person has been waiting to hear since the moment they met us.

CHAPTER 29

SINS OF THE FATHERS (IV)

When I was seven years old, my father took me to the Canadian wilderness to fish for walleye and pike with my grandfather. Several days into the trip the black flies and long portages along with my grandfather's anger were consuming us. My father's failure to catch any fish, accompanied by my slow learning, frustrated my grandfather. He threw his fish knife onto the rocks next to the lake. I would not bait the worm because I was afraid of the blood and the hook and the slithering and the slime.

"That's what's wrong with this world. You have to be tough. Nobody respects toughness anymore. You can't learn anything if you ain't tough. And you certainly can't learn to fish if you ain't tough."

"Lay off, Dad," my father said to my grandfather.

"You were just like him when you were a boy. Didn't ever want to do work. Didn't ever want to go to church. Girly. Couldn't catch a fish. You have to make him a fisherman."

"What does fishing and hunting have to do with being a man?"

"Everything. It's got everything to do with it. You should know this. You're a preacher."

"That's enough, Dad."

And just like that, we left. My father packed our things into our truck, and we drove all the way through the night until we reached home. My dad hardly spoke to me the whole way home and didn't explain why we'd left. His anger filled the cab of our pickup truck like an open sore.

"Why did we leave?"

"Quiet!" he snapped.

I sat rigid in my seat. Then his tone softened. "I'm too tired for talk right now, son. Why don't you read your book?"

Hundreds of miles across Michigan, Wisconsin, and back to Minnesota I read stories. When it got dark my father flicked the high beams into the night, watching for the golden eyes of white-tailed deer in the headlights. I took a flashlight out of my backpack and kept on reading, turning page after page until the words blurred together and I fell asleep with my face pressed against the moist passenger-side window of the pickup truck, being rattled awake at every pothole in the road.

CHAPTER 30

———————◇———————

TENDING THE GARDEN

"Dad, I need help. I think I'm dying. I snorted too much morphine, and I can't tell if I'm breathing any more."

"Listen to my voice. There is nothing to be afraid of. Take a deep breath."

I was silent on the other end of the telephone. I heard my father's breathing but couldn't feel my own.

"Can you hear me? Everything will be okay. I'm coming to get you. Stay on the phone with me."

And that was all it took. My dad drove seven hours from Michigan to Chicago and packed my entire apartment into the same pickup truck we had driven from Minneapolis to Chicago after I had graduated from Bethel. I was twenty-three years old.

He helped me scrub my apartment carpets and walls. He helped me clean drapes damaged from too many parties gone wrong. He bought me a warm dinner at a local diner down the street. He negotiated with my landlord and cut a lease buyout check. He never once scolded me. He didn't ask me a single question. And he rolled a joint for us when we got inside the pickup truck to leave for Michigan.

I watched his fingers roll the joint. I watched him lick the edges of the paper and crush the tiny leaves with the butt of his lighter. I watched him smile.

"Might as well put the past behind us. How about it?"

"No kidding," I said.

"You're going to live at the cabin next to Grandpa on the land. He's the one who bought you out of your apartment lease. You're going to have to do some work for him to pay the money back. You can clean up, get sober, and get your act together. No questions asked. Between you and me, your mother has been worried sick about you, and she's had enough pressure put on her because of the men in this family. So do her a favor and stay away from drugs." My dad took a long hit off the joint.

"Like pot?"

He coughed a cloud of smoke and then paused, holding his finger in the air, and then he coughed some more and then some more.

"Just be responsible," he said from the back of his throat, wheezing. "Stay away from the hard stuff." He handed the joint to me.

I chuckled.

"Does Mom know you smoke yet?"

"Sometimes you make exceptions for each other. A little grass goes a long way in surviving difficult times. It's a misunderstood substance. I use it respectfully. Your mom and I have an understanding about it."

I took a hit.

"So why did you ever quit smoking after college?" I spoke while holding smoke in my lungs, clenching my diaphragm and trying to talk at the same time.

I passed the joint to my father.

"Being an adult is tricky," my dad said, taking another hit and holding the smoke in his chest. "When I was a kid you could only be certain things when you grew up. Bankers. Lawyers. Pastors. Doctors. Things like that. Nobody ever told me to stay true to myself or follow my dreams. Being a pastor was the closest thing I could find to getting paid to be a spiritual teacher. It's easy to lose your sense of identity along the way. I used to get paranoid when I smoked all the time. I always wanted to be a writer. But I didn't have self-control back then."

"You're on microphone," I said.

"What?" He expelled a cumulous cloud of smoke.

"You're holding the joint and talking for a long time. You have to take a hit and then pass it right away."

"Oh," he said. He looked at the joint for a minute. He was stoned. "We called it Bogart—'Don't Bogart that joint'—because Humphrey Bogart always let his cigarettes hang from his lip for a long time."

We both stared blankly into space. The truck was a haze. I was thinking about something else and had forgotten my dad was holding the joint.

"So did you ever do any other drugs?" I asked.

"I tried most everything at least once," my dad said. "The only ones that ever felt compatible were marijuana and LSD. But I saw so many friends lose their minds to LSD that I stopped using it."

"Like acid?" I asked. "You did acid?"

My father stared at me.

"Bogart," I said to my dad. I started snapping my fingers. "Hit the joint, Dad."

"Right," he said. "Acid." Then he took a hit. He inhaled and then started coughing while he spoke. "Yeah. One time me and my friends did acid in the back forty on Grandpa's land when I was in college. Everything was perfect until Grandpa showed up on his tractor and made us work with chain saws."

He passed me the joint.

"Did you freak out? I would have freaked the fuck out, man."

"Oh, yeah. We lost it, man. But it was real eye opening. Like karma or something. He was shouting and looked like a machine. I mean, it was like he wasn't human. He scared the shit out of us, man."

I sat in silence for a long time, the joint hanging from my lip.

"What should I do next, Dad? Like with my life?"

"What do you want to do with your life?"

"The only thing I like so far is writing."

"You know, my old university has a great English department," my dad said. "It's just down the road from the cottage by an hour. Why don't you look into it right after you pass me that joint."

The summer had just begun, and soon after I arrived to live next door to my grandfather in our family cottage on eighty acres of rural Michigan woodland, I was accepted into graduate school down the road at my father's first university. I would study creative writing and "get my shit together." My father and I reasoned that by living alone in the cottage and focusing on graduate studies I might get clean.

The first night at the cottage by myself, the backyard was filled with fireflies. A mysterious breeze swam through the air, like ocean currents through the night sky. I smoked a cigarette under the moon. Compelled by something inside me, just like the wind, I walked through a field of country wildflowers. In the starlight the reds and yellows and oranges all looked white. As I walked, I trailed my fingers across their petals.

I walked through the pumpkin patch, freshly planted. And I walked through my grandfather's apple orchards, tapping the small buds with my fingers, and finally to the trout pond.

I lay on the bridge next to the artesian well and for a moment, near the sounds of splashing and the occasional swat of a rainbow fin on top of the water or bull frogs croaking and insects scurrying across my hands, I almost fell asleep. But something kept me. A small jerk. Like someone pulling me out of the water.

Walking the trail back to the cottage, I could almost hear my grandfather's boasting voice at holiday family dinners telling the story around the supper table: "And I pulled you right out of that pond [he points with his finger out the kitchen window at the trout pond]. You sank like a rock. You couldn't swim, so I pulled you out by your suspenders."

Later that night I woke in bed to the sounds of screaming in the forest. I sat up and threw my quilt to the floor. I listened again for the scream.

"*Mrrrreeee keeeee,*" it came.

I put on my boots and took a flashlight into the woods.

"*Mrrrreeee keeeee,*" it came again.

I followed the squeal down a small two-track path from my house to the dirt road and mailbox.

"Mrrrreeee keeeee."

The sky was dark and the moon nestled between clouds. The stars were gone. Then I heard the sound of three shotgun blasts.

Ka-blam.

Ka-blam, ka-blam.

I shined my flashlight at the barbed wire fence along my grandfather's property line and saw the white tail of a deer scampering off into the night. It had only three quarters of a right hind leg. In the taut hooks of the wire hung the bloody stump and hoof of the deer's leg. In the darkness across the road, somewhere in the ditch, I heard my grandfather talking to himself.

"Bugger me," he said.

Then I heard him groaning and wheezing as he climbed up the side of the ditch. Something about him made me feel unusually compassionate. I was afraid to announce my presence by shining the flashlight or calling out to him.

When I returned home my telephone rang. It was my grandfather.

"I need help. Glad you're living here now and all, but I hurt my hip. Come over and help Grandpa heat up that sack of corn kernels. I can't do it alone anymore."

"I'll be right there," I said.

He sat in his underwear on a kitchen chair, holding a frozen sack of peas to his hip. "Heat them kernels up for Grandpa." And so I heated the cloth sack of kernels and then massaged them onto his hip while he grimaced and whined. The sun rose over the tops of the pine trees outside. I saw the trout pond and the artesian well from the kitchen window.

"You fell in that pond," my grandpa said. He pointed at the pond.

"Yes, I know," I said. "You remind me about it every time I visit."

"Well. You did. You sank like a rock." He changed topics. "You know I had porcupine needles stuck in me one time, Adam," he said. "Had to pull them out. You have to be tough to pull a nail out of your own skin."

"That's pretty tough," I said.

"Now go into that cupboard and get me my morphine patch," he said.

"But Gramps, aren't you supposed to take those at night?"

"I take them when I need them," he snapped. "Now hand that patch to Grandpa and stop asking questions."

At the site of a cupboard stocked full of opiates from my grandmother's battle with cancer (she had died while I was in college) and my grandfather's various back problems and surgeries, I felt tempted to get high again. Within twenty-four hours I began a regular habit of stealing opiates from my grandfather's medicine cupboard. I split wood near the pole building and helped my grandfather in the vegetable gardens, watering the plants and hanging human hair in nets to keep the animals away. Then I got high before the end of the day. Each evening while my grandfather took his pain medication in the public of his kitchen, wheezing in his underwear after a day of working, I took mine behind the closed doors of his bathroom, licking the coating off pills, crushing and snorting the powder.

"Aren't you ever going to stop working?" I asked my grandfather one time during dinner when I was particularly high. "You're always out on your tractor in the sun, and you have a bad back. Maybe you wouldn't need the pain pills if you stopped working so much."

"It keeps me alive," he said. "Gotta be tough. There's always more to be done. You have to keep the land under your control—otherwise it goes wild on you. The doctor says it's good for me to take them pills. That doctor is a man of God, too. Goes to the church and hunts on my land during deer season."

Although I was using drugs again, without the constant company of women and parties, it didn't take me long to realize opiates increased my pain instead of easing it. In the wilderness at the cottage I watched deer eating in my backyard and listened to crickets and birds and coyotes at night. It was like returning full circle to the wilderness of Minnesota and to my childhood. The forest seemed as untouched as it was when I was a boy. The healing effect started off like a whisper. Like somebody was saying something to me that I couldn't quite hear. At first I would turn around, inside myself, and ask, "What did you say?" But nobody would answer. Then one night it grew louder.

"They're mushrooms," my friend said to me. "It's like pot, man."

"I don't know," I said. "Pot makes me paranoid these days. I'm trying to get off drugs."

"This will open your mind," he said. It was my first time having a psychedelic trip.

One of my friends lay on his back on the porch. My other buddy sat inside the cottage on my couch, listening to the stereo. As I walked through the field of flowers behind the cottage I noticed a birdbath statue of St. Francis. He looked like he was watching me or waiting for me to say something. The tips of the flowers blossomed into different colors: red, blue, pink, green, yellow, and purple. The blossoms wilted and then sprouted and blossomed all over again. Then I sat down at the foot of St. Francis. The statue glowed as if it were on fire. Then it spoke: "I am the birds and trees. Tend your garden," he said to me. "Tend your garden."

I looked at my fingers in front of my face. They melted. I saw cracks and pores on every inch of my skin. Each pore had something to say. Every grain of my flesh had something to contribute. *I am your hands, alive and separate. Where do my hands end and my arms begin?* A wave of jubilation swept over me. My body was fascinating. Each piece and body part was separate but connected. Each part with a unique personality and life story. I fingered the scar on my left arm. It ran from my elbow to my shoulder. Touching it I could hear the sound of my bone breaking into the cold ground at Bethel years ago. I touched the fingers of my once paralyzed hand.

While each of my friends were equally fascinated by his own inner workings, one of them was crawling across the grass on his hands and knees, examining each leaf and blade of grass, picking up small bugs on his fingernails while exclaiming, "You should see this bug, man!"

I walked into the cottage and examined the contents of my bedroom. In my bookshelves I saw myself emulating people and trying to be something I wasn't, trying to adopt other people's personalities. I saw religious confusion and the search for meaning, for somebody to tell me what to do to feel happy and safe. In my cologne and toiletries I saw fear of my father and grandfather and fear of other men. In my closet I saw shame in my clothing. I saw maiming myself with mean words in vanity mirrors. I saw a frightened child in my pillow case cover. When I touched my stomach I felt drug and opiate addiction. Then I heard the voice of St. Francis again, a kinder voice than the ones I had grown to fear, telling me to perform strange rituals:

Put this piece of clothing under your armpit and this one on top of your head. Put this pair of pants on with that jacket. Things you've never worn. Love them on your body. Transform your self-esteem. Now spray this cologne on top of that one and smell the combination. What does that mean? Now take your sheets and spread them on the floor. Now place your clothing on the floor and lay in the center. Bring that candle and light it. Say your grandfather's name. Now say the name of the boy who molested you. Jason. Forgive Jason. Where did Jason learn to play boyfriend and girlfriend in the first place? Think nice things about Jason. Now say your father's name. Now say your name. Now say the name of the women you've slept with. Try to remember. Say their names with kindness. Repeat each one a few times.

When one of my friends walked in and found me with a winter jacket wrapped around my head, scarves tied around layers of pants and shirts, candles lit and smelling like a cocktail of cologne, and muttering the names of women, I must have looked insane. But to me I was accomplishing something profound. I felt nauseous and crawled to the bathroom to vomit.

"I think he's having a bad trip," one of my friends said.

"I'm a butterfly," I said. I heaved into the toilet. "Everything is fine." And although I meant it, I could tell that my friends did not understand what was happening to me.

"How fucked up are you?"

"Fucked up?" I said, wiping my face with a towel. "Hardly fucked up. I'm awake. I have to quit using drugs. I have so much work to do. I have to tend my garden." I kept rambling.

"You know medicine men used to take people on vision quests with mushrooms," one of my friends said, ignoring me. He stood near one of my father's bookshelves, paging through a book about shamanism. "Hey, is this your *dad's* book?"

CHAPTER 31

○————————○

DRY HEAVING

As I continued my healing work with Carlos in various yoga studios, I realized the only thing keeping me on my back and curled into the fetal position during ceremonies was fear. I feared the experience of leaving my body, so it was time to sit up for an entire ceremony. Increasingly, my ayahuasca experiences were teaching me to heal myself instead of relying on anybody else to do it for me.

For most of my thirtieth ceremony I remember being rocked by visions like tidal waves. I pounded my fists on my knees and lifted my head whenever it fell down. Colors off the spectrum raced like drag strip fireballs, and I would find my forehead pressed against my thighs, begging out little sobs under my breath, "Please. Help me to stay in my chair. Please."

"*Vámonos,*" Carlos said, suddenly appearing in my visions.

I saw Carlos riding on the back of a golden eagle, soaring through a forest. I followed him, zipping through trees with giant butterfly cocoons hanging from their branches, the cocoons birthing out diamond rainbow moths and insects the color of God, zipping and singing, fairies and planets orbiting around fallen trees in the rivers, rivers made from memories. As I flew, I trailed my fingers lightly across the mercury images of my life. Faces and moments. Holding on to the arms of my chair back in the studio and focusing on my breathing.

Carlos flew high above me on the back of the golden eagle. The golden eagle screamed a sonic boom and Carlos pointed at me. I saw layered visions of my past.

Beer cans scattered across the carpet, hundreds of them. Empty bottles lying on their sides, vodka in small puddles on the kitchen floor. Ketchup on the walls. Mayonnaise smiley face melting on the wall. Syrup dripping out of the mouth of my VCR. CDs broken in half, scattered like smudgy rainbow scales on the carpet. Carpet smelling like beer. Foam. Hole the size of an ass in the drywall. Toothpaste on the doorknobs. Vomit in the bathroom sink. Girl from India, parents own elephants, your parents really own elephants? Kind of remember her, passed out still in the tub. Line chef from work passed out naked in the closet. Deck of cards ripped in shreds and floating in the fish tank. Lava lamp broken, slime on the floor, the purple water gone. The slime's just white-looking now.

My head is throbbing on the side, and there is a knot on my skull that looks like three marbles in a cluster. Someone pounded my head against the iron bar on my futon three times in a row. Manager from work. He piledrove me, and he ripped the strings off my guitar. Yeah. I remember that. There's blood on the collar of my shirt. He was laughing. Didn't even have a reason. Was just playing. That's what he'd said. I vomited and fell asleep under my bed. Locked myself in my bedroom. Fist hole in the door. Someone tried to get in.

Credit card statements are lying on my desk. Five, six, seven thousand gone. White powder on a mirror still, just a few crumbs. Pills in bottles. Stick the powder on my finger. Lick the powder on my finger. Feel a quick lightning burst of pain in my nostrils, a jet stream of blood falls from one nostril. It's dawn. Pinkish cotton candy, and the wind chill is near zero.

Police came and made people leave at some point. Remember a waitress from work was arrested for possession of marijuana. That's right. Blunts. We rolled nine and shotgunned for a long time. God, that felt like hours. Someone punched me in the testicles while I was hitting. I pissed blood and cried secretly in the bathroom with a joint in my hand the whole time. Wouldn't put the joint down. God. I was so stoned. Then methadone.

And dancing. God, the dancing was fantastic. That one kid, the Irish guy, he drank an entire bottle of the gold flake stuff and passed out face first into my entertainment center. Glass is broken. Glass in his face. He's laughing and bloody. My apartment is trashed. Someone is in my sleeping bag on the porch still. It's cold out there.

Cleaning. Wake everyone up. A few swigs of vodka. Wake up. Walking on the carpet. Be careful of glass. Glass. Smells like acid in her mouth. That meth-head girl. I made her leave after she blew me. Her boyfriend brought the drugs. I couldn't stand her following me around all night after I came. Where was he, anyway? Don't know how I came. I think I did. She tried to hit me, and some girl grabbed her throat and then they threw her out of my apartment. Can't buy from that guy again. She was swearing and cursing and swinging her purse.

Where's my pipe? Cologne is broken on the floor, and it hurts my nose to go near it, like a fresh arrow up into my brain.

My damage deposit isn't going to help this mess. Oh, God. Head hurts like hell. I need to get out of Chicago. . . .

Then, again, in the trees I heard a sonic boom from the golden eagle. I woke from the visions of my past. Feathers and a *chakapa* shivered over the crown of my skull. It was black in the studio. I heard the trill of children singing. Time slowed down. I felt the wind from the jungle somewhere far away.

Remotely, I lifted my head again from my lap and sat upright in my chair. Then I heard Carlos say, *"Cuerpecito."* Then I felt the breath of hot *mapacho* smoke on my face and a rush of feathers again across my eyebrows.

"Good job, my Christian friend. You're learning to find Jesus inside of you," Carlos said. "You're learning to be strong in your heart. That's true religion. Following that Jesus energy, that Christ inside of you, is a very difficult practice. Requires attention and awareness. Requires staying put. You can't force it. You can't find happiness with drugs and sex. Those are only temporary solutions."

I dry heaved for the next hour straight. Although nothing solid came out of me, each dry heave was a release. Every time I doubled over in my chair, I saw unfruitful attempts to create happiness. It had never been about getting high and feeling good. It had never been about freedom and self-expression. It had been about trying to take personal happiness by storm, and nothing real had come of it. My brute efforts had chafed me.

I dry heaved until the breaking of dawn, at which point something brand-new appeared. Something *real* announced its presence to me like the blast of a trumpet and the raising of a white banner. Still sitting in my chair at the end of the ceremony, unmoved, I

could feel my breath more intimately than I had ever felt it before. It was blissful. More precious than any material possession
and moving in and out of me like the wind behind tall and lofty
sails, it had always been there, seated firmly, guiding me: the breath
of life.

CHAPTER 32

A NEW COVENANT

While my buddy and I sat in the wildflowers behind the cottage, a chain saw droned in the distance. The sky was a mix of swirling faces and clouds. The ground breathed. I sat weaving the stems of flowers together into a crown.

"Hard to imagine people working right now," my friend said. "It's Sunday."

"That's my grandfather for you," I said.

We had swallowed enough mescaline to make the earth into a private wonderland. We talked as if we were treading water, sitting cross-legged, our heads poking above the flowers. For miles around us there was nothing but sky and dirt roads and rolling hills and forest. Our feet were dirty and bare.

Only months after eating mushrooms in my backyard I gave up drinking, smoking, opiates, pills, sleeping medication, and casual sex as if a night breeze had slipped through my window and carried each of them away. I no longer had any interest in self-destruction. Instead I spent hours every night in the cottage, reading by candlelight the ancient ways of shamans and medicine men, volumes from my father's bookshelf once kept secret in his study. I found myself smiling when I stumbled across old legends from my childhood, stories my father had told me inside the tepee at night. In particular I studied every indigenous tradition that had once upon a time used visionary plants like mushrooms or peyote.

As our conversation deepened in the field of flowers, we spoke about our families and in particular our fathers.

"I feel like I'm always going out *from* and returning *to* my father. It's like physics. It feels like natural law, like gravity," my friend said.

"Yeah, but each time we go back to our family, we've made choices that affect the nature of our family identity. It's like we're always changing our family and our family is always changing us. So it's evolution, not entropy."

"Ok. So what happens if a family gets sick? How does a family get sick and how do you heal a family?" my friend asked.

Then we were quiet for a long time, just sitting there in the flowers together. If I closed my eyes, the colors and my emotions and thoughts poured into each other like water. I could hear birds chirping.

A truck door slammed.

"Oh, Jesus," I said. "That's my grandpa." We stood on our knees and looked across the tops of the petals and blossoms. My grandfather walked toward us but didn't see us in the flowers. Then, as if the force of gravity reversed and pulled the apple back onto the tree, I stood up so that my grandpa could see me. My friend crouched on the earth and put his hands over his head.

"What are you doing in the flowers? Get out of there. Stop being lazy. It's two in the afternoon. Grandpa needs help splitting wood. I've got chain saws in the truck. Let's go."

When I saw him he was a machine just as my father had described (when *he* had done acid in the back forty). I saw armor instead of skin. I heard hissing instead of words, steam instead of emotion, and I smelled exhaust from his footfall. And then, "Grandpa can't do this by himself. Please, Adam. Grandpa needs your help." I heard squeaking and rusty iron against iron. Needing so much more than help.

"I can't work today," I said.

"Why not? You're lying in a field of flowers like a little girl. Now, listen to me. I lent you money. You owe Grandpa your time. Do you hear me?"

"We worked all week. It's Sunday, Grandpa. We're not going to work anymore."

In my vision his armor began to crack. I saw the first beams of light peak out from underneath. *From what hidden place of courage had my words come from?* He began to shake in front of me, standing heavier and heavier on the grass until it looked like the earth might reach up and swallow him.

"I should take you out of my will," he said. He spit on the ground. His voice shook. "I will take back every last one of them government savings bonds I've got for you in the deposit box."

"Like my father? Like you threatened my dad when he was my age? And how many times did *your father* threaten you like this? And *his father*? And his father's father? How long should we do this to each other? You tell me right now, you sorry son of a bitch. What do you want from me? I owe you a lot more than splitting wood, don't I?"

He choked up. "I'm getting too old to work like this, Adam. That's why I need your help. I can't keep up with the land anymore. It'll grow wild if I don't teach someone the right way."

"Here's some help, Grandpa. Try giving up. Why don't you stop working? What is there to accomplish anymore? Enjoy your old age. Try it."

A note rang forward like a horse. I saw white light pouring out of the top of his head for a moment, and then it disappeared and the colors were gone, and he was no longer the machine.

"Ok. I'll be done for the day now. Grandpa needs to take his pain medication anyhow. I was only asking because my back hurts, and I can't do it by myself. I didn't mean to rile you up. You're right, it's Sunday."

The encounter with my grandfather had been a generational reenactment of my father's psychedelic experience on the same plot of family land, but the outcome had been different from that of my father's encounter. To me it felt as though something truly miraculous had occurred. Although my initial urge was to immediately share my experience with my father, I was afraid he would no longer approve of psychedelics. Even though he smoked a little grass now and then, would he trust that psychedelics had actually helped me?

But they had. The very first time I had tried to use drugs again after taking mushrooms with my friends had been an utter disaster. After snorting enough OxyContin to kill a small animal, while driving the quarter mile from my grandfather's house back to the cottage, I ran my jeep into a ditch and woke up to a bloody nose. I started to panic. I couldn't feel my breathing again, like the time I had overdosed in Chicago, and I was afraid I finally had done it: I was going to die. Still in the truck with a bloody nose, beginning to hyperventilate, I realized that painkillers were actually, not just metaphorically, killing me. I longed for the feeling of my body and my emotions.

I had my chance. I knew this was coming. I should have listened, I thought to myself. Somehow in the panic, I was able to stumble out of the jeep. The front window was shattered. I leaned against it, seated on the cold, wet ground. I looked at my hands. At my feet. I was alive. Still numb, but alive. Ashamed—*How had it come to this?*— but still alive. *How can I confront my family again? They will know I got high again when they see the jeep.*

In a whiteout state of opiation, I concocted a scheme to earn enough money to run away forever. In a haze I stumbled to my grandfather's house and called the police to report a burglary. My grandfather was eating supper at the local diner up the road. I robbed his medicine cabinet of every last pill in order to make thousands of dollars. I would sell his drugs and hit the road. I could walk across the United States and bring a notebook. I would call my parents to tell them I was okay, just soul searching. I would leave my possessions like Jesus. *Let the dead bury the dead. I will pay everybody back later,* I thought. *Grandpa doesn't need those pain pills anyway. He's just as addicted as I am.*

When I spoke to the 911 operator I told her I had arrived at my grandfather's house to find the door open.

"I'm not sure if anything is missing yet. Have to wait until my grandfather gets home. Better send somebody right away."

Then I loaded up my backpack with my grandfather's pain medication. He kept a whole chest that he illegally backordered. He was taking as many pills as he wanted and filling his prescription at will. In truth, my grandfather, outside his doctor's orders, was self-medicating more than I was. The only difference was that I snorted twice a day and he took pills three to four times a day.

When the police and my grandfather arrived, they could not find anything missing. My grandfather did not think to check his medicine cabinet. "You sure nothing is missing? You checked through everything?" I asked. My hope was that he would find his medicine missing and receive some kind of insurance money after filing a police report. It was a lame brain attempt to steal without stealing. Simply stealing the money and leaving would have been smarter. Too snowed to think straight, it was as if something subconscious betrayed my plan to skip town.

"Nothing is gone," my grandfather said to the officer. "Must have left the door open by mistake."

"You're positive, Grandpa?"

"I'd like to speak with you alone," the trooper said to me. "Let's leave your grandpa and take a walk."

In the privacy of the wildflower field behind the cottage, the trooper confronted me and accused me of filing a false police report. "You took something and you wanted to pass it off like a burglary. That's the truth, isn't it?"

"Are you pressing charges?"

"No, but I will after you fail a lie detector test."

"I don't have to take one," I said.

"No, you don't," he said. "But how's that going to look?"

"What is this? Fucking *Law and Order*?" I asked.

"Watch your language, young man."

I was standing next to the garden statue of St. Francis. I couldn't feel my entire body. I was only getting higher, and it suddenly occurred to me that I did something crazy. I did something illegal. I was a criminal.

"You're pretty nervous," he said.

And just like that I fell to pieces. I sobbed out my entire story, from start to finish (and who knows what start and what finish that was, really), like a backyard confessional booth for a little boy, and I begged the officer to let me get sober and go free. The more I talked, the weaker my legs got, until I fell down in front of the statue of St. Francis, pleading. The officer crouched next to me.

"Why don't we go and tell your grandfather the truth, huh? He's a good man. He'll understand."

When it was all said and done I sat in the kitchen with my grandfather. He stripped down to his underwear as usual and asked me to fetch him a pain pill. He refused to press charges, but the officer charged me with filing a false police report anyway. Then the officer made me share my opiate addiction with my grandfather.

"So you take these, too?" He shook a bottle of pills in his hand.

"I have been for a long time," I said.

"They're addictive," he said. "They're bad for you."

"Then why do you take them all the time?"

"Gramps has to. I have a subscription."

"You mean prescription."

"That's what I said, subscription. I've been saying this all along. Saying how your dad should have taken you out fishing and hunting when you were a boy. No good growing up in the city. You aren't a hard worker. Your dad knows better. He's a preacher after all. You're lucky I'm going to get you out of this. You will owe it to me. I will call the sheriff, David, and he'll call the county prosecutor. They'll do us the favor because they know *I'm* straight. I donate money to the church. You know that? I bought a chandelier for the fellowship hall. Boy," he paused, "what a mess. What are we going to do about you?"

"So that's the whole story," I told my dad. "I've been clean for months since that night with the state trooper, except for psychedelics, which I'm telling you are very different from opiates. They're like psychotherapy for me; I'm telling you the truth."

I explained to my father how it wasn't about getting high, how it had become a serious thing, and how I had locked myself into the cottage bathroom to withdraw from opiates, three times in the course of a month, several times relapsing and repeating the withdrawal process. I would vomit and sweat and shake and moan. I would hear voices. I would lay my head at the base of the porcelain toilet bowl and talk to people who weren't really in the room. I would sleep the first night fine, almost die the second day in the bathroom, and by day three I was back to normal. I explained to my dad that I never would have seen the need to clean myself up without the mushroom trip. It had been so deeply healing.

He was quiet on the other end of the telephone. I could tell he was doing more than listening. He was thinking.

"I write stories and songs now, Dad. I go for walks. It's been keeping me clean and helping me stay off drugs, and I've only used psychedelics a few times, like three times. They open my mind. I don't feel any craving to use them, either. I mean they got you into the ministry, didn't they? And Grandpa was just like that today when I saw him. Just like you described him, like a machine. And he tried to make me work just like he made you guys work. He had chain saws and everything, just like you said. So you know I'm not lying about this. I swear to you that mushrooms gave me the courage to get off drugs. I relapsed a few times, but I kept going. That's what counts. I'd been using for over a year, you know? It's hard work. That last breakdown with the police officer was exactly what I needed, and I'm sorry I've never told you."

"Okay, okay. I believe you," my dad said. "I'm just thinking."

I waited.

"Tell me what happened with Grandpa today in finer detail," he finally said.

And when I told him about saying "no" to my grandfather while on mescaline, refusing to work for him, the vision of light pouring out from underneath his machinelike body, my dad finally said, "I know what you're talking about. It's been years for me, but I still remember. Do you have any of that stuff left?"

I didn't know how to respond right away. I hadn't been expecting such an immediate interest from my father. As a kid, I had seen the tepees and canoes, sure, the feathers and bones, and listened to my dad's myths and legends, but I had never known anything about the private psychedelic experiences that had first inspired my father to explore the universe and to part ways with his family's fundamentalist heritage.

The first night my father and I took psychedelics together we walked into the woods behind the cottage to take an ancient Mazatec herb called *Salvia divinorum*. Mazatec shamans used the herb to guide patients into important healing visions. The legal herb had been gaining popularity in psychedelic drug communities around the United States, mostly because it was incredibly potent and available for purchase at any local head shop. Like all of my first psychedelic inquiries, I had been experimenting with *Salvia* recreationally.

We came to a hole in the ground underneath a big sycamore tree.

It was deep and wide enough to fit several people. It was spring-time. Stars covered the sky. We decided my father would partake. I kept watch.

"This will be good for me," my dad said.

"It can be a little scary," I said, trying to prepare my dad for a possible "bad trip." "Best to keep an open mind and just go with whatever comes up."

"Just don't let me wander around. Make me stay in this hole," he said, as he made his way down into the deep crevice.

"It only lasts ten minutes," I said. "You'll be fine. Take three deep hits from the pipe."

He pinched the leaves into the pipe. His fingers moved slowly. He was afraid. His breathing was irregular. He looked up at me. I stood on the precipice of the hole. He handed me the pipe. "Could you load it?"

"Sure," I said.

Then when he was ready, he lay on his back in the hole and took three hits from the pipe. After the second hit he turned onto his side and coughed violently and spat on the ground.

"One more," I said.

After he took his third hit, his head sank back, his fingers opened, and he dropped the pipe. For a minute there was only silence, and his fingers twitched and his left leg shook with several tremors.

"Okay," he said. "I get it. I see it."

Then he tried to climb out of the hole in the ground. "Teeth," he said. "I'm trying. I can't keep up like this."

Then he fell back into the hole. "Help!" His eyes bulged out of his head and his hands stretched out into the night. "Help me, please, help me!"

I walked down into the hole and stood over him. "You're okay,"

I said. "Everything is good. Everything is fine, Dad." I put my hand on his shoulder.

He pointed at my face.

"Bear," he said. "Look at the bear." Then he toppled onto his stomach and began to whimper.

Then he was quiet. I watched his breathing. A few minutes later he returned.

"How was it?"

"I saw my life," he said. "I climbed to a white house on the top of a hill. The house was perfect, surrounded by a fence that looked like teeth. The teeth . . . I wanted to get into the yard to sleep, but the teeth were trying to eat me. I was afraid," he said.

As we walked back to the cottage, he added, "There was a bear up in the sky."

I almost told my father he had pointed at my face, and I almost reminded him of the birth totem he had given me, the small pewter statue at the altar of Lydia, but instead I kept it to myself and said, "You were trying to get out of the pit. It seemed important."

"I'm tired of being a pastor," my dad said. "Just until your sister is done with college. I hope I can last. I feel like I'm losing touch with reality. I need some time for myself. I wish more people accepted these experiences. They're truly mystical and very healing. You know this is the kind of thing that first inspired me to be a preacher, right?"

It was only weeks later that I booked a plane ticket to northwesternmost Peru, to the Amazon outpost city of Iquitos, and traveled twenty-four hours upriver, from a ferry boat to dugout canoes, and into the jungle to drink ayahuasca for the first time. I was still just twenty-three years old.

The inspiration happened while I was sitting in the bathtub one night in the cottage. I heard a strange sound in the backyard and walked outside wearing only a towel around my waist. The moon was crescent, and at the edge of the forest I saw the dark shape of a large animal peering at me. In the sword beams of moonlight through the branches and stumps and trunks, I saw a black bear. The bear snorted. I couldn't move. We stood looking at each other for several moments. Then, as if the bear meant to say something, it lifted one paw into the air and stamped it back down again lightly, like it was dusting itself off. Then it turned around and walked away, with little crashes and twig snaps, into the forest again.

When I returned inside the cottage I watched an adventure program on television. The program featured an ayahuasca ceremony and a group of indigenous shamans and their young American apprentice, Ethan. A bridge was being built from one culture and tradition to another, an old life to something new. I knew that I would go.

CHAPTER 33

BELIEVE IN YOUR HEART

A POST-CEREMONY JOURNAL ENTRY

The light of the candles is steady and pure. It's raining in the city, outside the yoga studio. Tonight was my fortieth ceremony. Makes me miss the jungle. I haven't had rain for a ceremony since my very first one upriver at El Puma Negro. I'm still seeing visions right now, but they're tame and peaceful. There are mythical creatures, like angels or deep-sea watchers. I can't see them, but I can hear them singing. It's almost like *icaro* songs, but not *icaros* from the Amazon.

The universe is so strange and beautiful. I feel lucky to know death and spirit this intimately, to feel humbled and still have so much life to live. I'm acutely aware of the mystery of my existence, and I feel thankful for that inspiration. When I was a kid people used to say, "All you have to do is believe in your heart, and you will be saved." Even though I know it's spiteful I almost wish I could make certain people drink ayahuasca, if only just once to see what it means to honestly *believe in your heart*. Some angry and childish part of me would say, "Drink this cup of medicine and try to tell me your fear-based point of view without purging. (Funny how imagining myself barking at somebody is making me feel very nauseated right now.)

Yet I still feel that I have these epic declarations to make about life and the universe. I can't tell where the evangelical motivation is coming from or how to speak of it without cutting somebody else down. I envy Martin Luther for having something as tangible as the doors of the Catholic Church to nail his theses upon. Funny to think that perhaps even journaling has been stripped of its cathartic power by Internet blogs and the confessional box of the creative nonfiction genre.

If I had to make a list of my faith statements, if I had no other door to nail them to but the door of my own heart, no other place to write them down but my own private journal, I would say . . .

When we believe in our heart we express ourselves from a place of unconditional acceptance. Unconditional acceptance will make every hell into heaven. This message of salvation is always meant for the here and now. Belief in the heart does not make life eternal. It makes eternal life heavenly.

The more we contemplate the physical organ of the heart, the easier it is to understand what "believe in your heart" actually means.

The human heart beats itself.

We don't know what makes a heart beat other than the fact that it beats itself.

We don't know why it starts beating or when it will stop beating.

The fact is that no matter what we do, good or bad, responsible or irresponsible, our heart nourishes us by continuing to beat itself. It is always sustaining us. Therefore the heart does not have a concept of judgment. It flows with whatever we choose and continues to support us.

All human darkness comes from feeling judged even though we are never judged.

The sun is the heart of our solar system.

No matter what happens on planet Earth the sun continues to shine upon us, rising and setting.

At night, the moon waxes and wanes.

The moon's light is a reflection of the sun's light.

No matter what happens, the sustaining rhythm of the heart is present.

The heart cannot pass judgment because its nature is rhythm. That's all the heart does. It lives and beats.

Believing in your heart means that *you are your heart*.

Your heart is part of the *one heart*.

Believing in your heart is not something you do because you feel you are wrong or bad or lost.

You are never lost, because you have always been present and experiencing every step of your journey.

There is nothing to accomplish for the sake of the heart. The heart is all there is.

Behind every moment you think you are not peaceful or feel dissatisfied, the ability you have to feel that way in the first place is always enabled by your heart. You can learn to see this when you feel afraid or find yourself in any type of place you don't want to be. Connect to your heart and breathe.

When Jesus talked about believing in your heart, he was not talking about belief in some "thing." Jesus was not talking about believing really hard that a mountain would drop into the sea or believing really hard that he died for your sins. Anybody who has stared hard enough at a cup and tried to believe it into floating has realized that this kind of believing doesn't work. Instead, Jesus proclaimed that the larger our belief in the heart becomes, the more we extend our sense of identity into the larger heart of the universe, which is God.

A miracle is a perception a person has while awakening to the universal heart.

Like many other miracle workers, Jesus always emphasized that miracles are meaningless because they extend from the exact same heart that sustains everything, whether it is a miracle or not.

Miracles happen all the time when you believe in the heart, because the heart is the miracle.

CHAPTER 34

ALPHA AND OMEGA

Blood dripped from my father's arms onto the white tiles. He sat with his back against the wall, crunched up next to the toilet bowl. He clenched the knife in his hand. I could see that he was getting brain shivers again. Like watching someone get the shakes, but inside his head. Like I could almost see his chattering thoughts and sensory data grating back and forth. His body trembled like a dead leaf in the wind.

"Am I okay?" His face was full of tears and sweat and saliva.

My whole life I had wanted to see my father vulnerable. I had wanted to see my father's soft belly. I wanted to see him without answers and afraid. I wanted to see his religion fail. I wanted to see him needing me, needing my love and affection. Needing a relationship with me that was not based upon a sense of duty. But in that bathroom I felt afraid for him. Seeing him broken and shivering on the floor, arms cut and bleeding, I wanted to demand that healing be easier, that he be given a break, a little bit of grace.

"It's so heavy," he said. His voice was a distant whisper, a rumble of thunder, miles away over quiet fields. Peaceful. Almost gone.

"You're right. It is heavy," I echoed. Water dripped in a soft beat from the shower head. I thought of every moment of darkness from the jungle. I thought of the noises at night and the shamans sitting quietly in their rockers until dawn, guiding me.

"Does it ever get lighter?"

"I believe that it does, yes."

"What should I do? I'm so afraid. Here, you should have this." He handed me his hunting knife.

"See. You know what to do already. Just one step at a time, Dad."

"Do you love me?" he asked me.

"Of course," I said. "Do you love *me*?"

"So much," my dad said. He sat up and grabbed me by the shoulders. He pulled me into his body and pressed his face into my chest. He cried so hard his foot shook inadvertently. Then he doubled over and began to vomit. To somebody else, maybe it looked like he might die. Really freak out. Lose it completely. Lost. But what I saw was different. I saw redemption and letting go. I saw release and freedom. I saw the heavens open up, and I watched soul-rain. A deluge. A volcano. A hurricane. A tidal wave. Then finally a resting human avalanche. And who can judge the way the mountains crumble?

Later that afternoon my dad committed himself to a psychiatric hospital. Despite my courage in the bathroom I was too afraid to visit my father in the hospital. As soon as he committed himself, I was captured by a fever that came and went for three days. I was twenty-four years old.

When my father returned from the hospital he canceled his trip to Peru to drink ayahuasca, which was the reason he had quit taking his antidepressants in the first place. Several months later he resigned from his job as a Methodist pastor.

When I moved to New York after another graduate degree, he came to visit me at my apartment in Brooklyn. I was twenty-seven years old. We spent his first day in the city at Ellis Island, where the first immigrants had landed in America. As we walked the halls together we paused to look at pictures of fathers and sons, mothers and daughters, farmers and workers with dirty faces and eyes filled with hope.

"You know, my breakdown was just what I needed to get out of the church," he said to me. We stood in the records room together. It was quiet. "It might sound weird, but I feel like the ayahuasca medicine spirits helped me. Of course, I would still like to go to the jungle one day and drink in actual ceremonies," he told me. "One step at a time, right?"

CHAPTER 35

ART THERAPY

PICKING UP THE PIECES

Nowadays I work at a Manhattan-based Franciscan residence home for the poor and mentally ill. (I can't help seeing the backyard statue of St. Francis in my mind's eye each day I take the subway to my office.) I'm twenty-eight years old. I'm a case worker and activities therapist for eighty adult schizophrenics. I also manage the personal budgets of all the residents in the building.

My job was given to me by a psychiatrist I met in an ayahuasca ceremony. Before the ceremony we talked together in the mesa, and he asked me, "What do you fear the most about drinking ayahuasca?"

"There are so many voices in my head already," I said. "I feel schizophrenic trying to integrate these teachings back home. Or like my culture is schizophrenic. I've developed some good disciplines, but it's hard. Not too many people take me seriously when I talk about ayahuasca."

"Have you ever known a schizophrenic?"

"No," I said. "Maybe myself at certain points."

"We're all a little bit crazy," he said. "But schizophrenia is an entirely different subject. Very misunderstood. I work with schizophrenics full-time in Manhattan. But you would be good with them, I think. You're very sensitive."

Halfway through the ayahuasca ceremony that night, during the full strength of its effects, he turned to me and said, "I think I might have a job for you in New York. Let's talk in the morning."

On Thursdays I take the residents to the movie theater, on Wednesdays I teach a meditation class, and on Tuesday afternoons I lead a St. Francis Friends of the Poor newspaper group. My newspaper is admittedly subjective. Instead of having the residents write stories about life at the residence home or the local community in Chelsea, like a real newspaper might, I invite the residents to share their life stories and insights. My newspaper group is secretly a storytelling group.

When we meet together in the art room I ask for quotes. The other day I asked, "So what are you afraid of?"

My residents said things like, "Spiders, heights, and snakes." Others said more reflective things like, "dreams of my father and aliens," or "I'm afraid to die alone," or "I'm afraid that God will get me while I'm sleeping."

Recently one of my residents, named Martin, brought his autobiography to the writing group. It was called *My Journey to the Light*. The fifty-page linear chronology of his life is a survival story that dwarfs most I know and is more poetic in its honesty than any poet I've ever read. He asked me if I could edit the pages that felt too "wishy-washy" or "whiny."

"I don't want to come across as selfish," he said.

"You're probably asking the wrong person." I didn't dare touch his manuscript.

One night not too long ago, while I was working in my office after hours, another resident named Janette knocked on my door to complain about Martin.

"He's screaming again in his room. I can't handle it," she said. "It makes me crazy. He's not the only one living here."

When I found Martin in his room he was pacing back and forth. He wore an angry look on his face. His eyes were fierce behind a pair of Coke-bottle glasses.

"It's not schizophrenia," he said to me. "It's a demonic entity." He held his finger in the air as a matter of fact. Then he came at me in two big steps, looked me right in the eyes, and said, "This darn voice keeps telling me to do things. That's why I yell, because I can't let it take control. I have to fight. It comes back more angry than ever before if I take medications. It's because of the chemicals."

"But the medications calm you down," I said. "Remember how calm you were at the hospital?"

"Look here. I have to exorcise this entity. It's a demon, and it's not going away by medication. Why don't you believe me? I suppose you think I'm crazy?"

"I do believe you. You're brave," I said. "I've seen an exorcism before in the rain forest. I've visited with shamans in the Amazon. They do some pretty intense healing work. I know you're not crazy."

"Can you perform these exorcisms?"

"No," I said. "I'm not a shaman."

"Well I need an exorcism," he said.

"But when your psychiatrist arranged an appointment with a shaman you changed your mind at the last minute. You wouldn't go."

"I don't recall that," he said.

"Okay. Well, if you're not going to take medicine, then do you want me to look into some holistic healing options for you?"

"No. I don't want anything. I know how to deal with this thing," he said.

Every time Martin tells me stories about his "entity" at newspaper group, I look him in the eyes. I make sure he knows I don't think he is crazy, even if he always refuses to accept help or medicine.

This past week Martin was admitted to the hospital again for another psychiatric meltdown. At our staff meeting, I asked, "Any word on how Martin is doing?"

"Apparently his sodium drops too low every time they give him an antipsychotic," one of the resident psychiatrists said.

"Maybe he really has a demon," I said.

"He's never going to get better without medicine," the nurse said. "He's got a chronic mental illness."

"Maybe so," I said. "But who knows."

"Well, take him to the jungle with you if you've got all the answers," the nurse retorted. "Since you and Dr. Stevens don't believe in medications anymore. You know he reduced some of his patients' dosages after he came back from the Amazon? Big religious conversion you guys must have had, getting high down there in the jungle."

"Look, I'm just saying that maybe Martin needs our optimism, along with his psych meds. I never said that I'm against medication."

"I've been here fifteen years," she snapped back. "I've been around the block, kid. I'm just being realistic. You can't heal schizophrenia."

"Maybe, and maybe not," I said.

RETURNING THE ELDERS

A JOURNAL ENTRY FROM MY FATHER

Dear Son,

It was emotionally difficult for me to read the final manuscript of your book, and so I'm sorry it's taken me so long to respond to it. However, the good news is that I've felt like journaling for the first time in a couple of years. I had thrown away all of my sermons, after I left the ministry, and I haven't written much ever since. I'm still amazed by the fact that your book was accepted for publication on the same day I returned home from the Amazon. It's a good book. It's come a long way, and I think the healing journey will resonate with many people who read it. My recent journey to drink ayahuasca in Peru was incredible, as I've told you already. Reading your book after coming back added to my experience of ayahuasca. Thank you for introducing me to the ayahuasca medicine path. I want to

*share with you my first journal entry after returning from
South America, and after reading your book. . . .*

May 2009

I still remember the day I stood in front of the church, robed and in
pastoral mode, listening to the offertory music, gazing at the blue light
streaming in from the stained-glass window, Jesus with the sheep of
his pasture, and I finally heard God say to me, "You do not have to do
this any longer." I knew pastoral life was over for me. I had just returned from four days in a psychiatric facility, being protected from
cutting myself, seeing Jesus in the group of fellow crazies at the psych
ward, people I nicknamed along with myself as the "potentials," people who had been cut by life but who showed resilience and courage.

My wife drove me the long miles to the hospital to help admit
me. She visited me every day, reassuring me and nurturing my broken mind. I knew that it was the beginning of a new era and that I
no longer had to work so hard to understand, to live, or to simply
be. The doors of my perception were opened.

Before Adam's journey to Peru, I worried about his mental, physical
and spiritual health. He was suffering from multiple addictions and
unhealthy behavioral patterns, and his health was a constant source
of worry. I was uncertain he would survive. Then, a marked change;
he traveled to Peru to drink ayahuasca, the spirit vine, something
I'd never heard of and knew nothing about. He was different when
he returned, decidedly different. Shortly after he returned from his
second trip to Peru, I was in the bathroom one morning cutting

myself with my hunting knife. It was my intention to cut myself until I could feel something real. Adam sat with me and truly listened when I asked for his help that morning. It was the same day I admitted myself to the psychiatric hospital, what would end up being the catalyst for me to exit pastoral ministry.

Over the years, each time Adam returned from the Amazon he seemed more whole, renewed. I sensed he had been humbled by something enormous, and was respectful of the gift of his life. A prodigal of sorts, he returned to the center that he had wandered from, or perhaps never had. Our relationship, often rocky and combative, took on a new and fresh vibrancy, father and son, yet friends and fellow seekers. Over the course of his repeated trips to the Amazon, during the oxygen-fresh time of my exodus from pastoral ministry and entry into early retirement, I considered drinking from the sacramental cup of ayahuasca for the potential healing Adam spoke about, but my dependency on antidepressants disqualified me from participating. I read his writings eagerly, his experiential reflections and ponderings on the journeys of spirit he had taken, and I was struck by the inherent wisdom and intelligence of this exotic, yet earthy plant that held medicinal powers for such deep psychic purging. After successfully weaning off my antidepressants (going much more slowly, compared to my first attempt when I quit taking my medications cold turkey), I was ready to go to Peru.

On my ceremonial mat, deep in the Amazon, in the middle of my first ayahuasca ceremony, the darkness was so dark and thick I felt absorbed and disembodied. I called for Jesus to talk to me, to clean my soul. I asked him to place his hand on my shoulder and squeeze it, to ground me and keep me safe. But Jesus wanted me to travel. I felt his presence call me into a journey out of my body. The *icaros* pulled me from my frame, up to the ceiling of the ceremonial mesa, where I saw the star-studded universe unfold like azure diamonds, beckoning me to visit their vast regions. I felt afraid. I heard my son's voice say, "Dad, I'm right next to you, everything is going to be okay." I heard the moans and sobs, the purging of my fellow seekers, a cacophony of unfinished business.

During the ceremony a black, hideous monster continually poked and prodded me, taunting me. I put up with it until it was too much. I clutched the prayer beads dangling from the string on my neck and told my shit of a personal demon aloud to "fuck off." We fought in a place I can only describe as "outside time." Then, finally, I growled my demon out and into oblivion as I vomited out poisonous doctrines, disappointments, failure, envy, lust and hatred, then settling into fits of uncontrollable sobbing and then laughter, and more and more laughter and then gratitude.

The way home is a bit treacherous, I thought to myself.

As the *icaros* guided me in and out of my body throughout the night, I was taken on a healing voyage into my past. Chest-numbing anxiety and anger welled up and railed within me. Moral failure. Impression management. Bureaucracies. Hatred of my workaholic, absent father and my boiling disillusionment with God, the church, canned theology, and the seeming endless futility of all life: nothing but the ingredients of a thick and sour emotional stew.

I had always known the pattern of lasting and genuine spirituality: there are no shortcuts, no counterfeits, only the narrow path through darkness, purgatory, and self-hell to the light, to the personal resurrection. My darkest fear in ceremony was that my attempts at fathering were dismal at best, tainted by my conflicted dance of uncertainty and depression. Antidepressants had put me out of body and without form. I was morbidly preoccupied with worry that I was replicating the sins of my father, overlaying the lives of my children and wife with toxic waste.

Like dreams of memories, as the most unimaginable visions drove me deeper into hell, I saw myself struggling as a closet Universalist throughout my entire career. More than anything I had craved an immersion into complete honesty, imagining spiritual and intellectual holism, somewhere, perhaps just a satiating gulp away. A pastor's midlife crisis: I fantasized, imagining myself on a quest, an inner-archeological journey to discover a hidden hot springs that would cover me, transform me, heal me, and revitalize my soul. I saw my family. They suffered with me, watching me wrestle with my mid-age demons, mistaking honesty with rebellion, indulgence with exploration, betrayal with honesty, and witnessing my frailties and recoils as the demon-dogs of faith-loss swallowed me up. Yet I saw that my family had loved me and always chose to see the kernels of truth and spiritual evolution along my imperfect path.

As my purge continued, geometric patterns of plant life and deep forest intelligence, creatures steeped in wisdom and love cheered me on. A much needed vision of my family came to me and touched my face, telling me, "We love you, and we accept you."

I wept and moaned, following the *icaro* into the body of a yellow snake. She took me on a winding trip into the heart of an ancient forest culture, and I knew this people had long disappeared off the face of the earth. I saw their village, their crops. We plunged under the earth to a subterranean world where I saw their people's dead, lined in graves lovingly prepared and cared for. Sorrow welled up in me again, and I cried for the people of the world, for our common fears and the struggles we share over the inevitable, unsolvable riddles of life and death.

I felt like I was dying and remembered that I could cry out for help. I crawled on my belly across the mesa floor, all sense of space and dimension fuzzy and strange. I was lovingly received by a ceremonial helper in the mesa who bathed my head, my shoulders, my neck and face in cold water for a long time. In the murky, silhouetted half-light I got a glimpse of his face, a smiling, painted Peruvian warrior. I tried to get up, and he gently laughed and said, "No, no, mas agua, mas agua." He continued to bathe my head. I felt my arms, legs and face slowly reform on my bones, and I heard the silly laughter of the Amazon night birds, the humming of countless insects. As I purged myself relentlessly into the night, by morning I felt that I had come home for the first time in many, many years.

Now, at fifty-five years old, after surviving pastoral ministry and even adventuring into an ayahuasca ceremony, the ironies of life have me taking care of the father I have hated, resented, and am now finally learning to love. My father, a fiercely independent man, his cynicism fine-tuned during combat across the hills of Korea, his anger and unresolved fears nurtured in the teenage years of a Michigan potato farm under the Calvinistic sun of *his* father, and his father's fathers, his physical labor the only semblance of a hobby even into his old age, is now feeble and weak. He is humped over and shaky. All my years of fearing my father, of trying to please him and appease him are past and finally gone, released somewhere in the jungle night.

He appeared at my door recently. He had stumbled through the icy waters of a nearby creek, bloodied and delusional, having overdosed on sleeping medications and opiates, thinking his house had caved in, throwing all of his possessions out his windows and shattering the glass.

"The stadium's fallen apart," he said to me, with a crazy look on his face.

"What are you talking about, Dad?"

"The stadium caved in. The people are waiting for me to rebuild it. I'm going to have to rebuild it before everybody can come for the big show."

"Dad, are you confused?"

"I need penny nails and a hammer."

"Dad, your arms and legs are bleeding."

For the first time, instead of a delusional man I saw a warrior like me and my son and so many other men: a man not knowing how to let go of his tenacious grip on something only he could name.

When later in the hospital my father asked me to "Give me another morphine or put me out of my misery," I thought of my own breakdown, of my purging, and my own healing journey. "Everything will be all right, Dad," I said to my father. I thought of my son comforting me when I had contemplated taking my own life, when I was cutting myself just to feel something real. "You'll see, Dad. Everything is going to be fine," I said. It was the only thing I could think of to say at the moment, and it's now the only promise in which I feel eternally faithful.

When I left the hospital I returned to my father's house and cleaned the glass and swept the floors, preparing it for his homecoming. I scrubbed the kitchen and bathrooms. I washed my father's clothing. I lit a stick of sage to make the house smell good. Then I walked to the garden behind my father's pole building and began to work the soil, turning over the hard dirt and spreading fresh peat moss. Cold, damp, black soil. Making the garden new and ready for spring planting.

ABOUT THE AUTHOR

Originally from the Twin Cities of Minnesota, Adam Elenbaas holds an M.A. in creative writing from Central Michigan University and an MFA in creative nonfiction writing from Georgia College & State University. He lives in New York City and works as a case manager and activity therapist for adult schizophrenics at a single room occupancy. Elenbaas is also the associate director of Om Wellness, a holistic health practitioner certification program based in Manhattan, and one of the founding writers/contributing editors of *Reality Sandwich*, an online magazine. For more information, visit FishersOfMenBook.com.

ACKNOWLEDGMENTS

I want to thank my true love, my soul mate, and my best friend, Tatiana, for her faithfulness to me, and for all of her support with this book. My family for granting me permission to share some of our journey, for being courageous, for always forgiving each other, and for staying faithful through difficulty. My dad for his permission to share some of his childhood stories and for writing the epilogue. My sister Heidi for her spirit of optimism and for traveling to the jungle by herself. My mother for perseverance and for keeping an open heart. My dear friends: Kiah, Jonathan, Jeff, Rob, Donna, Tammy, Heidi, Matt, Vanne, Camilo, Shon, Roberto, Eric and Laura for all their love and fellowship. The Sacred College crew for good study and good singing! Jonathan Phillips for permission to use his creative words, "Healing Christian Wounds." The RealitySandwich editorial team for creative support. My M.A. and MFA faculty for the workshops, thesis committees, the heart, and the constant attention to detail. Martha Hicks for being an elder, a healer, and spiritual guide. The fathers and staff at St. Francis for their flexibility and support. Ken Jordan and Fred Jordan for their editorial mentorship. The shamans, roadmen, and keepers of the divine tradition of ayahuasca medicine, to the ayahuasca medicine itself, and to the Holy Spirit, Jesus Christ, and the loving and redemptive God of all creation. Thank you from my heart.